Heaven Wants to be Heard

To St. Joseph,
Protector of God's earthly family

Heaven Wants to be Heard

Dudley Plunkett

First published in 1997

Gracewing
Fowler Wright Books
2 Southern Avenue, Leominster
Herefordshire HR6 0QF

ISBN 0 85244 428 1

Typesetting by Action Typesetting Ltd,
Gloucester, GL1 1SP

Printed by Redwood Books,
Trowbridge, Wiltshire BA14 8RN

Contents

Preface

People are frequently heard to say that the Vatican should sell its art treasures to help the poor. However good the intention, I am agnostic about this particular idea since I dislike the notion of great works of religious art disappearing into bank vaults and private collections, and I am saddened by finding works of art intended for the glory of God languishing in secular museums. I also know that the vast queues outside the Vatican Museum contain people who will find inspiration in the treasures and buildings that they are about to see in an appropriate setting. This said, I am even more convinced that the Church has other treasures that it keeps in vaults and does not sufficiently exhibit. The Scriptures and the teaching of the Church on spirituality, on morality and on social affairs are riches that are poorly catalogued and displayed. Also, the spiritual treasures of prophetic messages from Mary, the Mother of God, through her many contemporary apparitions, are kept concealed out of an inopportune deference to contemporary secular values, when they should be being broadcast by every possible means to irradiate people's lives in the dreary, self-orientated materialism of the end of the twentieth century.

The part of this art-work on which this book principally focusses is generally very little known outside of a small group of people who are only now beginning to raise their voice, even in the Catholic Church. I hope to increase awareness of the nature, content and import of prophecy accepted by members of the Catholic community, though not yet in every case officially endorsed as authentic by the Church. It is of course necessary that prophets stand the test of scepticism. There have been many secular writers who have referred to a millennialist attitude, whereby over-heated prophetic utterances associated with the year 2000 were leading people astray. Such writers have tended to associate individuals of often quite apparent hysterical tendencies, or wholly deranged people like the head of the Japanese Aum cult or the adherents of the Solar Temple, with those living within the community of the Christian Church and loyal to its Scriptures. I want to deal with this subject plausibly but without the mocking attitude of the secular media, and instead recognise the overwhelming evidence that Heaven truly wants to be heard in our time, and is relying on some quite ordinary human beings as its messengers.

That Heaven might be speaking should not surprise a believer, and yet few have given evidence that they are listening. It may seem reassuring that the Church takes a sceptical line as it did, at least at first, with Joan of Arc's 'voices'. Yet this is the very point: there is ample historical testimony that saints have been divinely inspired, and that some of the best moments of the Church's history have been under the influence of inspired leaders. Where is that inspiration found today? I am claiming that, first, it is always there in Scripture, and so the key points of this book are framed around scriptural quotations. Second, there is the fidelity of the Church's teaching to the tradition passed on by the apostles. And, third, there are the pleadings and warnings of contemporary prophets who are guided by the mystical presence of the Virgin Mary, whose messages characteristically conclude with the words: 'Thank you for having responded to my call'.

These three elements may be likened to the three legs of a stool that give it stability. The first leg, Scripture, is recognised by all Christians, but is made into an exclusive principle by evangelical Protestants. Catholics, the Orthodox, and some Anglicans and other Christians, regard the apostolic tradition of the Church, the second leg, as essential for the fullness of revealed truth. And the contemporary prophets form a third leg, stabilising the other two by recalling the truths of Scripture and of Church tradition where these are in danger of being forgotten or misunderstood. They are a special aid in our times of division in the Christian churches and of widespread unbelief. Moreover, these three kinds of inspiration stem from one source: God's Holy Spirit. I am therefore saying, to believers and non-believers alike, that there are treasures of different kinds, and that these are the treasures that they should be demanding that the Church give away to those who are poor in spirit.

Acknowledgements

I am grateful to many friends, especially in the Medjugorje Network, with whom I have discussed aspects of this work. I received valuable comments and suggestions from Fr John McCaffery OFM, Mgr George Tüttő and Petroc Willey, and I feel a special debt of gratitude to Ken Smith for some advice he gave me on the very day his life suddenly ended during a day of prayer in honour of the Blessed Virgin Mary. And, as always with my writing, I thank my wife, Francine, for her fresh and wise observations.

1

'End times' prophecy in Catholic consciousness

Signs of the times

The heart of this nation has grown coarse, their ears are dull of hearing, and they have shut their eyes, for fear that they should see with their eyes, hear with their ears, understand with their heart, and be converted and be healed by me.

(Mt 13:15)[1]

Prophecy has always preoccupied religious writers, but it is doubtful whether most Christians appreciate either the extent of prophetic content in the Bible or the echoes of such prophecy in everyday Christian life. The mystical tradition of Christianity is widely ignored, and its return to the mainstream of religious consciousness is overdue if humanity is to understand with its heart, and be converted and healed. Needless to say, these concerns cannot even be addressed in secular thinking because prophecy and mystical phenomena take us into the realms of the spirit and of faith. When the Second Vatican Council (Vatican II) in the 1960's referred to the need to read the 'signs of the times' it was affirming that God, through his independent divine power, constantly leads human beings through their own experience and the events of the world to better recognise him and his as yet unrealised plans for creation.[2] It is a commonplace of this religious view of life that people should be alive to the goodness of the Creator as well as to the reality of the powers of evil. The contrast found between the powers of good and of evil encourages people to decide on a personal stance, for that is how life on earth takes on meaning and direction and, according to Christian belief, leads to life with God after death. In this sense, all religious thinking takes us beyond this present life, and is prophetic.

Why then do so many thinking people today, including the ablest of students of human history, refuse to see that there is any meaning, direction or ultimate purpose to human existence, or else want to represent it as reflecting only narrow or short-term interests? As examples, two very substantial recent historical works with the alluring titles *Millennium* (Fernandez-Armesto, 1996) and *Age of Extremes* (Hobsbawm, 1995) are both blind to the claims, let alone the truths of Christianity. The first asserts that history resembles 'a mosaic made by a monkey' (p.8); he is relativistic, and post-modern. In many ways his is an unusual work of history, deliberately picking up interesting but relatively unknown aspects or phenomena, but the exercise seems pointless in the end. Hobsbawm is ideologically motivated, denying anything other than a materialist view of history. In a 600–page book he deals with the decline of religion in half a page (p.337). There is a grudging acknowledgement of Catholic social teaching (p.114), while Polish attachment to the Church is portrayed as nationalist and anti-Soviet, and the liberation of Poland from Communism is described with only a glancing reference to the 'increasingly aggressive Church' (p.476). In other words, there is no understanding of the place of faith and of the Church in European history, nor any recognition that such a role might still exist. This book describes the current state of the world as a 'global fog' (p. 558). The book concludes in this state of puzzlement, but with the sense that things must change. Neither of these historians gives a fair account of the Christian contribution to civilisation, and both omit any reference to the Christian understanding of humanity's journey on earth; it is hard to avoid the conclusion that 'they have shut their eyes, for fear that they should see'.

By way of contrast, Norman Davies' 1300–page tome, *Europe: a History* (Davies, 1996), painstakingly seeks to provide a purchase on events that is not random, post-modern or ideological. He ends his book with an assessment of the West's attempts to come to terms with the collapse of Communism in the Soviet Union:

> The present 'Europe', a creature of the Cold War, is inadequate to its task. The moral and political vision of the Community's founding fathers has almost been forgotten.
>
> (Davies, 1996, p. 1136)

He finds a greater sense of purpose in the East, especially in Poland, where the Church 'never submitted, as elsewhere, to political control ... and kept the loyalty of the proletariat, which in turn undermined the Party' (p.1107). He adds two interesting comments: that 'History must give the Poles the principal credit for bringing the Soviet bloc to its knees' (p. 1108); and that Pope John Paul II 'played a vital role in his native Poland, undermining Communism by sheer force of personality and his support for human rights' (p. 1079). These seem to be part of a much wider vision of history, one that combines the description of events with some hint of explanation through the analysis of psychological and ideological factors. That is to say he allows for human intentions and vision as motive forces. This is something that appears to me to be essential to any Christian understanding of the world. In a review of Davies' work Fernandez-Armesto revealed his hand:

> Nor is there any such thing as a common European culture. Christianity is something said to be its basis, but this extra-European religion has done far more, since arriving in Europe, to divide than unite us. (*The Times*, 7 October 1996)

It is not of course necessary for Christian believers to run to the other extreme, the fundamentalist assumption that God is guiding history according to the word of Scripture, and thus virtually take responsibility out of humanity's hands. Clifford Hill notes this tendency amongst some Evangelicals, and advances a more nuanced Christian position, namely that history is above all the working out of God's plan for humanity, whatever else may enter in (Hill, 1995). History can in this view be seen as at least including a train of events brought about by people seeking God's will by responding to signs of the times. In his work on Christian eschatology,

Jurgen Moltmann reconciles these two perspectives on human affairs. He speaks of hope as the eternal now. He suggests that history does not lead to eschatology, defined by him as 'the doctrine of Christian hope, which embraces both the object hoped for and also the hope inspired by it,' but that eschatology breaks in from beyond history (Moltmann, 1967, p. 16). This is a view of history from which a Christian can derive some genuine understanding, unlike the chance-based theory of a monkey's mosaic.

The original gospel occurrence of the phrase 'signs of the times' was in Jesus' reply to the Pharisees' request for a sign from Heaven to attest his authority. There are signs to read, Jesus says, and they should be able to read them just as they read the weather: 'In the evening you say: "It will be fine; there is a red sky".' But Jesus goes on to warn that, though his listeners can predict the weather, they fail to read much more important signs (Mt 16:3). Are things any different now, when innumerable commentators set out to interpret what is happening in political, economic, and social matters, without regard to the signs of where humanity stands on its spiritual journey? So many disable themselves at the start by not discerning the presence of God in creation, whereas Scripture asserts that we were made capable of knowing God through the use of reason.[3] Part of 'knowing God' is understanding how his will is manifested in the natural and human worlds. For many believers this is urgent at the present juncture, because they see the world as moving into a phase of 'end times', that is a new era that is bringing closer the time of divine judgement.

I do not want to take space here with a negative view of where we stand at the end of the twentieth century, but I am convinced that the Western world especially is morally and spiritually moribund, and that only a major religious revival can restore meaning to the life of a whole civilisation. This moral and spiritual collapse in relation to gospel values is what needs to be reversed through the spiritual renewal called for by the contemporary prophets that feature in this book. Indeed the remedies for these ills are contained in the Bible and in the messages of the prophets recalling its wisdom to us. It follows that, while my intention here is to give a reasonable account to any interested person of how the 'end times' suggested by such signs as these are viewed by prophets of Catholic inspiration, and more generally in Catholic consciousness, I would argue that the moral and spiritual disintegration of contemporary culture needs to be recognised by anyone who is sincerely trying to understand human experience. It is from an awareness of our human condition that we can see both the need for change, or in religious terms, conversion, and the starting-point for the journey back to moral wholeness - or, in spiritual terms, holiness.

In religious writing there have been many interpretations of our times as an apocalyptic age, but some writers in this field have undoubtedly emphasised the sensational, such as extravagant claims to secret knowledge of the future, so that it is hard to attend to inner truths the quoted prophets may be attesting.[4] I do not seek to promote such prophetic predictions, for it seems to me that any spiritual truth they contain is already there in Scripture to be grasped by everyone who cares to read discerningly. However, if I can persuade some sceptical readers to accept that hope is being dramatically renewed in our time, by a rich mystical and prophetic vein in Catholic consciousness that runs directly counter to dominant secular values, my efforts will have been well worth while.

Three currents of prophecy

> *He has let us know the mystery of his purpose, the hidden plan he so kindly made in Christ from the beginning to act upon when the times had run their course to the end ...*
> (Ep 1:9–10)

I believe that it is possible to find a striking convergence of three currents of prophetic teaching in the Catholic Church today that is not widely recognised. First, there is the teaching that is based upon sources in Scripture and the apostolic tradition of the Church that was confirmed and developed by the Second Vatican Council in the 1960's, but which is only now being understood and absorbed into Catholic life and thought. This teaching is being offered to the secular world as a contribution to thinking about human values and purposes. On these matters the Church understands its role as speaking for God, as a prophetic voice calling forth a civilisation of Christian love in calm tones that are still being heard, though with difficulty, above the storm of cultural innovation and dissonance.

The second current is the extraordinarily vital teaching of Pope John Paul II, who continually asserts the primacy of spiritual values, calling people back from atheism and materialism, especially by affirming the sanctity of human life as God's gift, and in his constant reflection on the values of justice, peace and love as God's will for the world. While some regard this teaching as a reversal of a trend set by Vatican II towards more open dialogue with the contemporary world, others see it as a concomitant of that teaching. What can be safely asserted is that it is official teaching of the Catholic Church which also reflects the distinctive personal contribution of John Paul II. This teaching has a highly counter-cultural character, seemingly pitting religious ideas against secular materialist forces. It is often represented as a battle between conservatives and liberals, between science and faith or even between a patriarchy and a radical women's movement. But it is equally possible that all of these conflicts mask a fundamental warfare of the spirit underlying the apparent phenomena, as the world struggles with issues of development, population control, relations between rich and poor societies, haves and have-nots, peace-making, ethics in the economy, sexuality and life issues, or scientific policy, and attempts to assert the dominance of its utilitarian values.

The third, perhaps more disconcerting current of prophecy is the belief in miraculous phenomena, events that are believed to be supernatural and coming directly from God, which are claimed to be occurring throughout the world at the present time. These include visions and messages of Jesus Christ and the Blessed Virgin Mary, interior promptings received by so-called 'locutionaries', weeping statues and icons, and many other happenings too numerous even to mention here, which believers are convinced are authentic, and which are bringing about a powerful spiritual renewal in those sectors of the Catholic Church in which they are given credence. Although not infrequent in history, such phenomena are a very marked feature of the twentieth century, a century when it might have been expected that scientific thinking and rationalism would have made it impossible for such claims to survive. However, millions of people are being drawn each year to the sites of these happenings, such as Fatima and Medjugorje, as well as to the traditional Marian shrines of Czestochowa, Lourdes, Guadalupe and many others.

What is less frequently emphasised than the numbers undertaking such pilgrimages is the content of the messages claimed to be being received from a heavenly source by the human intermediaries at these shrines, especially the modern ones of Fatima, where the Marian apparitions occurred during the first World War, and Medjugorje, where they began in 1981 and are still continuing. These messages concern God's plans for the world and its future. In Fatima, speaking to three young children in 1917, the Blessed Virgin prophesied the end of the first World War, the Communist revolution, the persecution of the Church, the outbreak of the second World War, the expansion of the Soviet Empire, and its final collapse. She also promised the conversion of Russia to Christianity, and her triumph, as the Immaculate Heart, over evil. Only the last two of these prophecies have still to be fulfilled. She announced a further grave calamity that would affect the Catholic Church, but no details of what she said have ever been confirmed publicly. It has been widely surmised that it has to do with the loss of faith and discipline among priests, and with consequent conflicts within the Church of the kind that are increasingly common today, eighty years later.

In Medjugorje, in Bosnia, the Blessed Virgin has been appearing daily since 1981 to several people, now nearly all in their thirties, and she has spoken insistently of the spiritual priorities of human life: the value of prayer, the need for faith in God and conversion of life, and the nature of peace as the acceptance of God's will, whether in people's personal lives or in society at large. Although the effect of these apparitions has spread throughout the world, and has brought about thousands of conversions to Christian belief, or to an intensification of Christian life, little general or media attention has been paid to the actual content of the messages given at Medjugorje, or through the many similar recent apparitions, for example in Spain, Rwanda, Japan, Venezuela, Ireland and Korea. Nor has it been observed how similar these sets of messages are to one another, in spite of the virtual impossibility of any mutual influence in the natural order of things. What is even more remarkable, when these messages from different parts of the world are examined as they will be in this book, is not only this convergence of content, in the appeals for spiritual values, for faith in God and reliance upon him for the solution to social, moral, and political impasses of our time, but also how closely these messages resemble teachings of the Pope.

John Paul II has continually suggested that our times should be seen as a 'new Advent' or preparation for the coming of the Lord, and has held his views consistently from at least the beginning of his pontificate.[5] Therefore, his teaching must be considered as independent of the various visionaries and prophets who have offered their messages to the Church during this period, and any convergence of content must be considered significant, and not contrived. Whatever is believed about the authenticity of mystical apparitions, some explanation must be sought for these similarities. Surely it can only be the Gospel that underlies their teachings, but which Heaven wants to be heard in a fresh way. There is no new revelation of religious doctrine, just the gradual manifestation and magnification of gospel truths by two instruments of God's will, the Virgin Mary who once said 'Let it be done unto me according to your word' and the Pope, who regards the Blessed Virgin as leading God's people back to him, and has inscribed in his papal coat of arms the motto 'Totus tuus', as the commitment of his life in loyalty to the Mother of God.

A prophetic tradition

Blessed be the Lord, the God of Israel! He has visited his people and redeemed them. He has raised up for us a mighty

> *Saviour in the House of David, his servant, even as he promised by the lips of holy men, those who were his prophets from of old.* (Lk 1:68–70)

In spite of the shortcomings that I am saying characterise the work of many of the best-known contemporary historians, this is not a historical work. In particular, I am not taking the time to look at how prophecy has been conceived over time, except in the sense that I underline the unique importance of prophecy in Scripture. In fact it could be said that the Bible has been too much analysed as history, and insufficiently as prophecy. Words taken from Scripture can carry the two kinds of interpretations, historical and prophetic, but biblical events are not simply things that happened, even when they appear to be, such as the stories of the patriarchs and the continual warfare of the Israelites. Infused into these accounts is also an understanding of God and his relationship with his chosen people. The behaviour of the Jewish people is both a working out of that relationship in particular lives and times, and also a myth or metaphor of much wider application from which we can learn in our own time.

Much of the Old Testament is a prophecy of the coming of the Messiah and a recording of the divine promises for the human race, far beyond the fortunes of the ancient Hebrews. When, on the road to Emmaus (Lk 23), Jesus explained the Scriptures to the two disciples, he referred to the prophetic character of the Law and the Prophets, in other words virtually the whole of the Old Testament. He constantly refers to the fulfilment of scriptural prophecies in his own life, and indeed the Gospels draw attention to several Old Testament prophecies fulfilled in the details of the life and death of Jesus, including the Saviour to be born to the royal line of King David, his betrayal by Judas, the casting of lots for his clothes, and the prophecies that he would be pierced by a sword, but would not have any of his bones broken (cf. Jn 18 and 19). Contemporary Catholic prophecy reiterates and confirms scriptural prophecy. It may well be that Heaven is making itself heard a second time to prompt humanity to a fuller understanding of God's word in the Bible, and especially in the interpretation of scriptural prophecy.

Contemporary prophecy, therefore, must be confirmed by some scriptural precedent if it is to be considered authentic. No Christian can contradict the Bible which reveals the existence of eternal life and eternal death. Salvation, or eternal life, is a matter of individual destiny, dependent upon the faithfulness of a person to their conscience and to the grace of God merited for everyone by the life, death and resurrection of the Redeemer, Jesus Christ. Although these teachings of Scripture cannot be revised, there are many questions about which we can seek independent clarification today such as, what help can we get to enable us to be saved? how can we know if end times or the collective 'end of the world' is near? or, how does God see the state of the world today in moral and spiritual terms? Some of these matters receive considerable attention from contemporary prophets.

To sum up, prophecy has been neglected, whereas it is both a vital part of Scripture and a gift of the Holy Spirit in our own times. It is the voice of Heaven calling for our attention. It is part of the evangelising mission of the Church to make this teaching known, all the more so because it has a ring of urgency and contemporary relevance about it. There are many signs that we are now living in the last times, when great spiritual outcomes will be decided. This is made clear in the most authenticated of contemporary prophecies, especially the messages of the Blessed Virgin Mary in Fatima which have been endorsed and developed in more recent prophetic messages from all over the globe. The overwhelming burden of these messages is that the mercy of God has been tried too far by the wilful disorder of humanity, and that his justice is soon to break forth. Already we seem to see harbingers of this in the trials being undergone in central Africa, the former Yugoslavia, and the countries of the former USSR. What do we learn about what God expects of the world today? In one sense it is what he has always expected, that people obey his commandments, that they love him and one another. But in another sense we are given to understand that he expects a specific and whole-hearted response on a number of fronts, particularly the honouring of human life from conception to the grave, the spiritual renewal of those who have lapsed from belief, the unity of the

Christian Churches under the spiritual primacy of the Bishop of Rome, the honouring of the Blessed Virgin Mary, and the reconciliation of warring parties in conflicts around the world.

Humanity is on trial in these matters. If those concerned do not respond, then a time of spiritual decision draws nearer, and perhaps will very soon take all initiative out of the hands of those who think they are in control of the world's affairs. This is what seems to be meant by the frequently occurring message that the present time of grace and mercy will be superseded by a time of justice in which humanity collectively will suffer 'chastisement'. God's mercy and justice are seen to be in a dynamic relationship to each other. He wants to show us his mercy, and constantly does so, even though we are undeserving. However, there can come a point when we have so consistently refused his mercy by our lack of repentance, that he is obliged to withhold it, and we must then suffer his justice. This reflects the Christian doctrine of judgement and the penalty of eternal death in hell. Far less 'just', because still merciful, is the threat of chastisement, or the pains of earthly suffering, which God allows to give everyone the chance to repent, and thus avoid eternal death. Any suffering in this life is therefore a mercy if it is calculated to bring us to God.

The nature of this chastisement is not clearly described, but it would be consistent with many passages of Scripture and with contemporary prophecies to identify Aids and other diseases as part of it, along with a variety of natural disasters, famines, human conflicts and conflagrations of a local or global nature. Chastisement is not definitive punishment; it has the character of a warning, and it is only if the warning is not heeded that God's justice would require the final rejection of sinful offenders. However, even in these extreme situations God wishes to respect our free will, and will never force us to conform. The responsibility rests with each individual. Nothing has changed from the original issuing of the ten Commandments. We are not robots; we are free to choose to obey or not out of the strength of our conviction, our conscience, or our love for the Creator.

Catholic consciousness

> *The man who prophesies talks to other people for their improvement, their encouragement and their consolation.*
>
> (1 Co 14:3)

What is Catholic consciousness? It is no doubt true that there is a culture of the Catholic Church that carries with it insights, modes of understanding, awarenesses and forms of communication that are distinctive. But this is not to say that the Church is homogeneous. On the contrary there are different networks in the Church community of such a kind that people can be persuaded that their thinking represents the mainstream, and they can be virtually unaware of alternative ideas. So it is that currents of thought and experience develop discretely, unsuspected, and often hardly come to light, though they may be of importance to a particular group which is being spiritually fed by them. The mystical strain in Catholic experience is of this kind - a reservoir of spiritual inspiration hidden from the eyes of most Catholics, let alone non-believers. Thus, the exemplary virtue, the spiritual insights and divine messages that have come to the Church through the saints and other holy people over the centuries have often been concealed for years, only becoming widely known after the death of the messenger. Examples, out of many that come to mind, are Therese Martin, who died in obscurity at the age of twenty-four in a Carmel in Lisieux, Marthe Robin, who spent fifty intense years of spiritual and apostolic activity lying ill in bed nourished only by communion wafers, and Matt Talbot, the reformed alcoholic who prayed the streets of Dublin.

However, in the communications revolution of our times, this traditional Catholic consciousness is being rapidly modified and expanded. Large numbers of people can share information through private editions of papers, newsletters, audio-cassettes and videos, and indeed Medjugorje information now circulates through the Internet, as well as through innumerable privately published newsletters, fax exchanges and informal associations, gatherings, pilgrimages, days of prayer, retreats and other networks. This communication process is having a distinct effect on the Church. It can run independently of mass circulation Press and broadcasting. While most are unaware of or ignore what is happening, others are informed, updated, and feel involved and inspired. This has been the way that information about numerous recent visions of the Blessed Virgin and their associated messages has circulated within the Catholic community along routes that never existed before, but which are proving marvellously adaptable to monitoring the prophetic voice which is bringing new encouragement and consolation.

A summary of the main claims of this writing

- the Bible announces God's plans, especially through the Old Testament prophets and the apocalyptic discourses of the Book of Revelation
- prophecy is a vital part of Scripture and a gift from Heaven for our times
- contemporary prophecy needs to be taken seriously, both because of the seriousness of the world's moral and spiritual condition and because God is showing us a way to spiritual renewal through his messengers
- discernment as to the authenticity of contemporary prophecy must involve comparison with the Bible
- certain current apparitions and messages of the Virgin Mary are key and virtually indisputable prophetic phenomena
- the prime message of all authentic contemporary, as of biblical prophecy, is 'peace, not disaster'
- prophecy is not prediction, and even where it refers to future events their occurrence, positive or negative, depends upon the spiritual content of as yet unrealised human decisions and actions
- prophets, biblical and contemporary, warn that if we do not respond to the message of God's mercy by a spiritual conversion we must expect his justice
- the Holy Spirit is already provoking widespread spiritual renewal in the Church, but all are called to change their lives before human power is humbled and divine power asserts itself definitively
- these claims articulate with the apostolic tradition of Catholic Church doctrine and practice, and the Christian obligation to make a response of love to the needs of the world in a time of spiritual and moral crisis

2

Personal and social choices of the 1990's

The need to examine our times

No one can be the slave of two masters: he will either hate the first and love the second, or treat the first with respect and the second with scorn. (Mt 6:24)

This book is woven from two main strands: evidence from the surrounding world, including insights that can be derived from personal experience, and the accumulating wisdom of the ages and sages in which I feel able to place my faith. Though I write as a Catholic who senses a profound spiritual renewal occurring in the Church, I also hope that I can open a dialogue with a reader's own knowledge, experience and beliefs. It seems to me regrettable that so few works of the present time attempt to combine a firm anthropology and a committed spirituality, for such works could speak of hope to believers and non-believers alike. I am concerned that so little is written that addresses these questions, and therefore cannot apologise for taking some space in this chapter to explain to the reader how my interest arose through the circumstances of my own life. Contemporary writing in Britain offers little that ponders moral values and spiritual meanings in relation to the cultural environment, though this has been a genre that has been immensely successful in the United States, where the very word 'culture' is highly marketable. In his best-selling interpretation of American culture, Allan Bloom, a man who stands in the Judeo-Christian tradition without being a believer, sees clearly what is being lost by the secularist movements and through their impact upon intellectual and cultural life: the culture of the United States intelligentsia is closing itself to ultimate truths and values (Bloom, 1988). What the present book is about is the related idea that there is today a significant moment in British religious culture, and perhaps in the whole of Western culture, that needs to be recognised and reflected upon, because it offers opportunities to our contemporaries that can otherwise pass us by.[6]

The impact on British culture of the change in values and lifestyles that occurred in the 1960's is well recognised. From that time a distinctive set of values spread throughout the world as a philosophy of individualism, an espousing of freedom of choice and a materialistic outlook. Whether one points to the relaxation of sexual moral standards, the emergence of a human rights movement in the areas of race, gender and sexuality, the student protest movement and its consequences for authority structures, or the new affluence of the young expressed in the fashion and music industries, evidence is not lacking that thirty years or so ago there was indeed a radical and seemingly irreversible shift. As a result of the resultant changes in values, mentality and social structure in the space of a few years, this period came to be seen as the modern cultural watershed. However, a generation has now passed, and much has happened since. We cannot continue to speak of our experience in Western society as if something that happened more than a generation ago is the main explanation for what we now think, are, or do. While acknowledging the cultural significance of that time, I want to try to understand better just what did happen, and also to suggest that even more significant cultural changes have subsequently occurred.

Moral and spiritual relativism

> *People will be avid for the latest novelty and collect themselves a whole series of teachers according to their own tastes ...*
>
> (2 Tm 4:3)

Contemporary culture supports those who declare their independence of the Deity and are offended by the notion that God might want their obedience, their service, their worship, or their conversion. Such 'liberated' individuals either deny God's existence, which allows them to make up their own creed for living, or they remodel him to fit their own need for self-respect, freedom or self-indulgence. In practice, they acknowledge a religion that assumes that the individual is a god, and that there is no other divinity than the self. That has been their solution to the problem of the 'two masters'. They have decided which to serve. For those unable to accept that their moral lives should be governed by any external authority, albeit exercised in the name of God, the most convenient philosophy to adopt is that of moral relativism, whereby the individual conscience aided by rational arguments is entitled to form its own judgement of right and wrong.[7] Many are those who have reached a point of personal revolt that leads them to repudiate any religious faith that they have ever held, or to express their faith in terms that at most concede the remote possibility of the existence of a divine being. What we consequently see around us is a progressive undermining of moral codes and spiritual convictions, a process through which any constant values have disappeared from view for most. Underlying all of these elements of contemporary culture there is a basic pretence. Promises are freely made, but none of them is kept, and yet the fraud is continued and even justified by an overarching secular credo.

The world today is very different from the way it was in the 1960's. Many more people now feel disenfranchised, subject to anonymous authority, unclear about the locus of decisions in society, appalled at the retreat of public institutions such as the family, the church or the school from any position of influence or as sources of hope. There are also many who feel hopeless, disillusioned, and stifled by oppressive forces that they cannot identify, but which prevent them from developing careers, building secure futures, or expressing their values effectively through a democratic process. I regard the thirty years since the late 1960's as a vast cultural experiment that is now being evaluated, and to a considerable extent questioned. I believe that the 1990's have been a time

The secular Credo

The Apostles' Creed has twelve 'articles', or sections. How might a secular version be expressed under the influence of a truth drug?

- We believe in wisdom, especially if it is of recent origin and can impress others
- We believe in science, but are equally fascinated by horror and superstition
- We believe in sophistication, that is, knowledge with prestige but no meaning
- We believe in seeking, but not in finding
- We believe in devotion to duty, except for persevering in marriage vows
- We believe in happiness, provided there is no serious discussion of the subject
- We believe in charity and humanitarianism, but not to the point of sacrifice
- We believe in human rights, but exclude the unborn and the terminally ill
- We believe in choice, and also in all manner of techniques of persuasion
- We believe in Western freedom, and its necessary price of controlling others
- We believe in finding out about things, except about our own souls and our sins
- We believe in belief, provided we are not ourselves asked to believe.

when the momentum of changes begun in the 1960's has seriously faltered. Not surprisingly, the span of a generation has allowed a new awareness to develop, but we are still too stuck in the conventional expressions of the old outlook to be able, like the proverbial fish, to see the waters in which we are swimming. I think that this is why we need to examine the values that dominate our times in a way that can be disturbing, even painful, so as not to lose the opportunity we have to see ourselves more objectively, and then to find a new will and purpose that can correspond to current needs and circumstances.

And yet, our times have seen the rebirth of a spiritual interest through the discovery of Eastern mysticism, and the development of a religious and philosophical consciousness that has become known as New Age, a form of neo-pagan spiritual belief that regards God as the totality of human aspirations to truth, harmony, and knowledge.[8] It is asserted that God is within, and can only be known from special insights into humanity and the natural world. All is God. All is good, and there is no sin, no guilt, no sacrifice, and no redemption. There is no obligation to a Creator. New Age spiritualities acknowledge no absolutes; all 'truths' are equal. Such neo-pagan ideas are increasingly common in America and Europe, and are accepted by many highly educated members of New Age sects who are dismissive of traditional Christian beliefs. In Britain there has been a clearly observable example of this in the dramatic impact on the town of Glastonbury of large numbers of New Age adherents, many of them with satanic and magical elements to their beliefs. Despite the presence of fifth century Christian remains and a shrine to the Blessed Virgin Mary claimed to the oldest north of the Alps, it is possible in Glastonbury today to indulge in all manner of occult interests, such as mind, body and spirit healing, earth mysteries, tarot, shamanism and contact with the dead.

It may be thought strange how very intelligent, and otherwise rational people can be seduced by the notion of a mysterious power available through esoteric knowledge, often through a cult, or through recourse to gurus, mediums, tarot cards, ouija boards, crystals, and so forth. The line dividing the occult from what is purely human invention is not very clear, but apart from those manifestations that might be generally agreed to be ugly, or maybe dangerous, or even evil and very dangerous, there is an aspect of New Age that is very compelling. It is self-glorifying, it has to do with what wonderful beings humans are. There is no personal God. The divine is within us, we are each divine, and each one has their own spiritual authority. It was hardly possible to live through the 1960's without being influenced by this New Age consciousness, whether through an interest in astrology, meditation, reincarnation, sexual liberation, care for the planet and environment, the peace movement, or through the emergence of new religious forms of a neo-pagan type or the sects and cults led by charismatic leaders or gurus.

These influences have touched very many lives, and have been used to undermine not only secularist ideologies but traditional religions as well, just as throughout the history of Western religion there has always been a gnostic tradition that contradicted the Christian teaching about the Fall and human redemption through the life, death and resurrection of Christ. This way of looking at reality becomes very profoundly anti-Christian. It subverts Christian beliefs, often turning symbols of Christianity upside down. Those who argue for such new teachings usually refer to new conditions, new knowledge, or new needs that have come about in today's world. Reliance upon an immanentist theology, even by some leaders in the churches who fear to speak clearly about the reality and the rights of the all-holy and wholly-other God has increased the likelihood that believers will embrace elements of New Age consciousness without realising what they are doing. Because of certain apparently positive aspects of these beliefs, and their prevailing optimism about the future, many Christians seek to incorporate them into their beliefs and practice. [9] This saps the integrity of, and brings confusion to those Christians who naively absorb superficially attractive pronouncements unrelated to Christian Revelation.

Examples of how influential such ideas are in the Christian churches are increasingly frequently encountered, for example in radical feminism, with its faith in the earth-mother myth and its ecological extension, and its notion of 'Woman-Church'. If we look at the spiritual life of the Church, there are obvious elements of New Age thinking that have come into established Church activities through spirituality workshops, retreats, meditation techniques, and the like.[10] Even more common are the claims from those who see themselves as oppressed by traditional moral teachings of the Church, and who base their spiritual approach on their opposition to any form of moral discrimination. The impact of such well-reported pressure-group activities is particularly powerful on the young, because they tap that aspect of the mentality of the young that wants swift change and universal contentment.[11] And, further, it helps to justify among the young the claim to greater licence for sexual behaviour, as if the only thing wrong about promiscuity was the existence of moral rules that forbid it. But perhaps, after all, this has been an unsurprising reaction to the extreme materialism of much of modern culture. Some are left thirsting for things of the spirit, but they are so corrupted by individualism that they hope for a spiritual dimension that can be tamed, that will make them into self-revered gods, justify their foibles and obsessions, and allow them to follow their whims in the name of a universal force that contains but does not constrain them.

A personal turning-point

Confess your sins ... (Jm 5:16)

It is certainly the case in my own life, as for many of my contemporaries, that the 1960's revolutionised many of my attitudes and values. I myself had been raised within a Christian tradition. I recall a Catholic boarding school education that entailed effort and cultivation of the mind within the context of a ghetto-like culture, which was all the more exclusive for being of a refined, middle-class variety. At the time I swallowed it whole as I did not know of any alternative. The religion I developed was well-informed in its own terms, pious, and with more than a touch of class-consciousness. It was several years before I could even challenge it. The friends I made were, I think, involved in the same pretences as I was. We did not dare to, or did not think to be anything else. During the 1960's I came to see this dedication to social and religious traditions as meaning blindness to changes in the world, including those affecting the Catholic Church.

My desire for work with some social impact eventually led me into voluntary work overseas, in an adult literacy programme in Bolivia, and this experience has stayed with me all my life; it was a direct acquaintance with poor people and a culture of poverty which gave me a sense of people's dignity whatever their circumstances in life. I then spent four years in doctoral studies in the United States, and there felt the full brunt of the 1960's cultural revolution. I encountered a progressive Catholicism, based largely upon secular democratic philosophy, and fuelled by a liberal Catholic Press offering a highly tendentious interpretation of the ideas then emerging from the Second Vatican Council. This approach fitted well with the academic world and with many of the new policies of the Kennedy and Johnson administrations, but from a Christian standpoint it raised the awkward question: what is the difference between a good professional person and a good Christian? Many of my friends felt deeply challenged by this issue. Gradually young priests and lay Catholic graduate students began to take a more and more independent line. Some of the priests left the Church; others sought release from their vows within the Church; and many of my Catholic student contemporaries lost their religious faith.

This contact with American Catholics who were angry about Church inaction on social and political issues, and who rejected much of the Church's moral teaching, affected me at a time when I was close to the American experience of the Peace Corps, the War against Poverty, and the Civil Rights movement, to say nothing of the Pill. The upshot was that, by 1967, both my wife and I had ceased any religious practice. Indeed, before long we had abandoned a religious view of life. At the time this seemed like a real gain, an emancipation from external authority experienced for the first time, and an essential step in our own personal development. Once I had decided that I was not going to continue being a Catholic, I found it impossible to give any serious thought to religious matters. I could not bring myself to enter a church. I felt strong animosity to clergy and Church hierarchies, and I saw my childhood and education as having conditioned me to passive submission to a system of values and ideas that no longer carried any credence. I resented all the energy I had put into religious practice, and I felt only relief that I could now search for what might really mean something to me at this stage of my life. I embraced a rational approach to human problems, and allowed it to stifle any remaining religious insights. This affected my relationships, my beliefs, my work, and my concept of society.

In 1968, when I returned to England to a university post, there was enormous ferment in universities around the world, and I felt strongly identified with the student movement. For several years I tried to find a new basis for my life in socialist thinking, in the rational use of the social sciences, and in humanitarian service to the causes of educational and social reform. My university career revolved around these notions, but did not satisfy me fundamentally, and I was seeking a meaning to my existence that did not simply reflect the expectations of others. My interpretation of the world tended more in a psychological than a political direction. This may have been as much through fear of the exposure of political action as because I saw results coming through the individual, but in the 1970's I gradually abandoned the political struggle in favour of a 'selfist' approach, one of cultural rebellion and self-assertion. Education became liberation, running parallel to therapy, the human growth movement, individualistic philosophy, and an opting out of more global responsibilities. This was a time of experimentation with relationships and philosophies, and with psychological movements such as encounter groups, co-counselling, Gestalt, est, and other explorations which I prefer not to recall too closely.

I had reached a very low ebb in my spiritual journey by the mid-1970's, at a time when I was to all appearances doing very well professionally. I spent several months on short missions for UNESCO working on educational projects in the Ivory Coast. The lifestyle of well-off expatriate aid personnel was materially rewarding but exploitative of others, and ultimately self-destructive. Seeing so many people wasting their time, achieving nothing and drawing large salaries from the UNESCO budget, was a corrupting experience, an education in selfishness. And although I continued to pretend to myself that I was steering my life by the ideal of making a contribution to human welfare, I was losing faith in any secular cause. Everything around me seemed to be compromise, hypocrisy, ulterior motives and lack of moral courage, and I felt the guilt and the corruption of all of it.

One positive feature of my life as a university lecturer, however, was that I took my teaching very seriously. I believe I contributed to my students' social awareness and personal development and helped mature students to return to study after periods of intellectual stagnation. I kept my own mind working and refocussing, and somehow I also kept my sense of wonder at the world, as I travelled, read, met people, and explored new forms of learning. Something was stirring within that experimental activity that did not seem on the surface to have any clear purpose. My attitude to Christianity, particularly to the Catholic Church, remained ambivalent. I saw the need for moral standards in the world, but resented any institution that sought to provide them. I felt alienated from the Church as a source of moral authority, yet I remained a student of Catholic teaching, both papal documents and alternative views, such as the liberal Dutch *New Catechism* which appeared at the end of the 1960's. I was aware of a position that was becoming increasingly influential in the Church at that time which combined openness to social and other secular sciences, a special leaning towards Jungian psychology, a liberal attitude to sexual morality and an enthusiasm for ecumenical and inter-faith links. I found that I went along with this philosophically as far as that was possible from outside the Church, but it had absolutely no attraction for me as a religion. That is, it did not bring me closer to spiritual awareness or give me any sense of belonging with Christians.

My eventual reconversion to religious belief and practice lies at the heart of this book and was, I believe undeniably, due to a personal experience of God's grace. In my searchings I thought that it might be valuable to read the New Testament to see whether there was any way in which I could still identify with Christian beliefs. In early 1983 I began with St Matthew's Gospel. I remember reading: 'Ask and you shall receive, seek and you shall find, knock and the door will be opened to you' (Mt 7:7). So desperately did I want to resolve my questions that I got up and knocked on the nearest door! Perhaps that was a turning point. Certainly in the succeeding days I found many passages of Scripture that moved me as I had never experienced with Scripture before. The words of Jesus spoken to Martha, 'Martha, Martha, you have so many cares, but few are necessary, indeed only one' (Lk 10:41), brought tears to my eyes, and yet I was still without faith.

One day, a few weeks later, I found myself in a street near

Westminster Cathedral in London. It was a church I had often visited in the past, but not for some twenty years. I wanted to find somewhere quiet where I could think about my life without distractions. I went into the Cathedral and walked down the right hand aisle towards the front, where I had often gone to confession in the past. In fact the confessional was still there, and there was even a red light showing to indicate that a priest was in attendance, and a small queue of penitents was waiting in line. I walked past them and sat in a seat in front of the Lady altar. It was peaceful. I wondered to myself whether there could ever be a time when I would once again take Christian faith seriously. I needed some surer values. My life was all over the place. I was far from happy. I felt guilty and worthless. And yet I remember having the thought that if I would ever accept Christian faith it would be in the remote future, when all these current worries had somehow been dealt with.

I had been vaguely aware that a service was being conducted at the altar in front of me, but I had paid no attention to it (I later came to know that it was the Evening Prayer of the Church). Then a reader came to the lectern and opened the book. A sudden thought came to me: 'What if he reads something that has a message for me?' This was such a clear and powerful idea that in spite of my instinctive resistance I prepared to listen attentively to the reading, which began: 'A reading from the letter of St James'. After that, I heard only one phrase, and then I was plunged into a profound world of awe as if the Almighty had addressed me with his own voice. I was trembling. I was no longer thinking. I was unconscious of my surroundings. I thought of how petty my troubles were, and how it was time to sort them out and get on with a proper life. The phrase I heard from the reading was its opening words: 'Confess your sins'. As soon as I could get my knees to work I stood up and joined the confessional queue.

Afterwards I walked away in a dream-like state. I felt shocked at what I had done. I asked myself if it was genuine, if I had not acted too impulsively, and if there was any way that I could actually translate into daily life the implications of having asked God's pardon for my sins. Rationally, psychologically, even sociologically, it seemed like a game or experiment. I had had a sudden meaningless regression that I would have to renounce in order to get back on course, to be normal. I had flipped, but I could forget it, repress it. And yet, at another level I knew with an utter certainty that what I had done had been right, and with each passing moment this certainty became clearer to me. I felt elated. I felt as though all the mess I had been ensnared in had suddenly been cut away. There wasn't a problem any more. I wasn't bound to the way of life I had been living. The Gospel was valid, and it showed me another way. Only one thing *was* necessary: to accept God's love.

The relevance of my experience to this book will I hope be obvious. I would not be writing it without the new faith I found in the mercy and the grace of God. I saw that these are offered through the gospel call to repentance and conversion. It was still some time before I became aware that this call is also made through the increasingly insistent messages of contemporary prophets, whose role it is to remind people of the challenge of their own consciences and of the life lived by Jesus Christ. Although it was the experience of an individual, I felt I learned a universal lesson from it, a lesson that can be absorbed by anyone, believer or not. In fact, when Malraux made his famous remark that either the twenty-first century would be spiritual or it would not be at all, I believe he had sensed this question of ultimate purpose as being one that would pose itself for our whole Western civilisation. We are being challenged in our history, in our beliefs, in our moral outlook, in our personal, communal and international relationships, to review individualism and materialism, the key features of the pragmatic philosophy of contemporary culture and, if I can use an old word in hopefully a new way, to *rededicate* ourselves through commitment to values and a way of life that will be both more human and more spiritual.

A century of broken promises

I looked from the altar gate, and saw the image of rival deity standing at the very entrance. (Ezk 8:5)

Since my own return to faith I have come to sense a widespread longing for wholeness, truth, love, and peace, not as a simplistic utopian wish, I believe, but as a genuine apprehension of human possibilities in the light of divine guidance and grace. The obviously human aspects of this intuition are the awareness of our spiritual roots, found often in the most secular discussions, the strength of our memories of personal innocence and its disruption, an enduring hope in the transcendent even if at times we deny God, a fervent wish for an ordering which we identify as much with the past as the future, and above all disillusionment with the world we have created out of our own desires. Related to this last point is the sense of hopelessness and directionlessness to be sensed in a world that has resolutely turned away from the Absolute. We can see this as brokenness in many facets of life, and we undoubtedly need to recognise the damage and the failure, if we are to kindle hope for the reversal of values that could lead to human and spiritual fulfilment.

Otherwise, the risk we run is of following false paths, just as the Israelites did when they worshipped false gods and sought an earthly kingdom. It was in fact on this feature that the mission of Jesus appeared to stumble when he was rejected for not conforming to the image of the expected messianic King. Just so today we choose 'rival deities', earthly creations and idols, or we worship our own rationality and its standards. Instead of the Hebrew Torah with its every 'jot and tittle', we now have political correctness. Or we defer to intolerant elites more concerned with status than justice. Instead of the High Priests, we have industrial or media moguls, and we observe governing groups imposing a self-sufficient and self-justifying leadership. Instead of Scribes and Pharisees, we have career politicians, and we see accommodations to other powers as the price for preserving our position from too radical questioning. Instead of the Herodian compromising of Jewish tradition, we have the false ecumenism of New Age Christians. The time has come to reappraise many of these creations of the laboratories of twentieth century culture.

All of this is against the backdrop of Scripture which repeatedly warns of the necessary consequences of deliberate evil. The truth proclaimed all along has been ignored: the prophets' burden of doom is recognised, but it is rarely understood as relevant to the present time. Collectively, the world's holy books present us with an image of humanity as living a brief expanse of life on its way to somewhere else, whether it be heaven, rebirth, or a depersonalised nirvana. However unknown or mysterious our destination, if we are on a journey we have to consider ourselves as pilgrims or exiles, but always in hope. Such images, so typical of religious sentiment and thinking, are unacceptable to secularists who are obliged to assert that this life is all that there is, and that consequently we have to get all we can out of it for ourselves and for our own. People with such values need to be optimists who look for a brighter future, of more money, a better job, the right partner, house, clothes, and so forth, or else they are obliged to despair, and to endorse suicide, euthanasia, abortion or other acts of destruction of human life. Spiritual transcendence and secular materialism are our two polarised options today. Not surprisingly, they are often represented in the Bible as the choice between life and death.

It may be thought contentious to claim that there is a widespread sense of emotional and spiritual exile, of nostalgia, of longing for innocence, of regret for the unsavoury living of our times. Too often when they are expressed these sentiments sound hypocritical, because they are voiced by people who are not willing to change their values and their behaviour, like St Augustine according to his celebrated phrase: 'Lord make me chaste, but not yet'. In many ways the century that is ending parallels the biblical experience of the ancient Israelites when they found themselves wandering in the desert for forty years, but still thinking of the melons and garlic that they had enjoyed while they were slaves in Egypt. Despite their law, and the holy covenant by which God offered them life, they repeatedly chose the 'death' of idolatry and the earthly kingdom of nationalism and power. This exile and the later one in Babylon, which brought about the destruction of all that they had achieved, stand as prophetic warnings, perhaps especially for today's Western world, of the need to recognise and return to the values and moral and spiritual truths of a lost civilisation, and to the faith which originally created it.

The fundamental options chosen by the dominant powers of the twentieth century have been secular and materialistic. These values, which at first seduced humanity by their glittering promises of wealth, freedom, scientific truth, technological transformations, the perfectibility of the human species, and many other blandishments, can be seen to have proved so elusive that we must now ask ourselves whether they were ever more than a mirage. People came to believe that life would continually get better, that wars were being fought to improve humanity's lot, that wealth and health would no longer be privileges of an elite but would be shared by progressively larger proportions of the human race. Yet, paradoxically, the century of so many scientific discoveries, technological change and self-analysis has left humanity as uncertain about any possible solutions or 'truths' as has ever been the case, thus lending respectability in our times to agnosticism, to pragmatic government, and to moral and spiritual relativism on a scale that has never existed before. Far from a perfected world, we see signs of one crumbling into fragments, as the beliefs and expectations of so many are seen to have been belied.

The hopes of peoples at the ends of the two World Wars, and even at the fall of Communism, have not been sustained. The values offered to incite humanity to belief in modern secular prophecies have proven deceptive, because they entailed manipulation and repression. Or they have been shown to be inconsistent, because they favoured specific sectors of society and were never as universal as they had pretended. Or they were simply empty, because they were the propaganda of the lying leaders of Nazism and Communism, or the illusory dream-worlds of free marketeers, gurus, advertisers, and so forth. People believed that they would find fulfilment as citizens in workers' democracies, identity as a nation or a race that was purified of foreign elements, or beauty and love through psychologically or cosmetically improved versions of themselves. They thought that they could prove themselves, that they could be independent of traditional authority and convention, that they could be free. But it was an illusion. They have ended up as puppets, unaware of the strings being used to control them, and of the many forms of mass betrayal and deceit practised in modern society.

Signs of fragmentation

It would be easy to catalogue the triumphs of moral and spiritual relativism that fill the media, but this would not be to my purpose. The point of recording them is to ensure that the book is more firmly dedicated to helping reverse or transform such features. The following are mentioned as an illustrative sampling, as signified by their alphabetical ordering:

- abortion, euthanasia and the culture of death
- blasphemy and discounting of spiritual values
- criminal mafias and drug cartels in several major nations
- disintegration of the two-parent family
- eugenic/embryo experimentation
- fundamentalist and sectarian violence and extremism
- gay marriage
- human rights violations, particularly of religious freedom
- inequalities of wealth within and between societies
- juvenile crime, drug use, and promiscuity
- loss of moral authority in society and in social institutions, especially schools
- moral protection of minors progressively diminished
- narcissism in fashion
- political and financial corruption and slease
- religious and psychological manipulation by sects
- sex tourism and pornography
- terrorism
- violence in entertainment, crime and political unrest and war
- world powers' weakness in dealing with repression, violence, and famine
- youth unemployment and marginalisation.

As time goes by, more and more desperate protests are made at the situation that has been created. The media provide doom-laden forecasts. Politicians seek new adversaries to blame. Scapegoats are summoned up. Fanciful remedies are sought in new policies, theories, even new religious doctrines, or rather old ones dressed in new clothes. No one can sort out any consensus. We have reached a point of near-anarchy. The sign of this is that almost no one is accorded trust or respect. A classic example is the sheer mischief of the media attack mounted in 1992 on Mother Teresa. Everyone is suspect, and subject to cynicism. Western civilisation is steadily subsiding into self-mockery and nihilism. Why should there be such a strong sense of foreboding, so much disgust with the way the world is organised, so little confidence that science, technology and government will find solutions to human problems, so much disillusionment with the standards of morality, with the level of integrity displayed by authorities and leaders, so much sheer hopelessness as evidenced by a breakdown of moral and spiritual order? Could it be that there is a need to recognise a situation close to utter despair before people of today will actually be able to find space for hope? Even space for faith? Europe has become almost wholly de-Christianised, the churches have lost influence, and economic and political ideologies have replaced the Christian consensus of former centuries. The dominant view today would likely be that we no longer need Christianity for identifying or securing social, political or economic objectives. In the contemporary crisis of values there is little sign that religious concerns are taken seriously into account.

The result of all these blind alleys and contradictions in contemporary culture is confusion, and any efforts to assert a positive direction are greeted by cynicism or satire. Instead of fulfilling its promise, the twentieth century has become the century of empty and broken promises. The century has been one-sided in its commitments, giving liberally to Caesar but very little to God, and the sense of a collapse of the spiritual is now endemic. The abandonment of God has been so complete that contemporary society is blind and deaf as regards the truths about the origins and destiny of humanity which were always the deep concern of earlier civilisations. In fact there is a polarisation between a minority religious view that hopes beyond the rational, and a secular view that believes only in the resources under rational control. The latter view has greater economic and political power associated with it, and is succeeding in turning the world into a spiritual desert, with people so overwhelmed that even believers are unable to react. The churches cannot defend themselves, because they can find few spokespersons to advocate any alternative to secular values. Believers have become inward-looking within their communities, and to all intents and purposes agnostic in their behaviour. That is to say that, at least in much of the Western world, there is denial of God in any practical sense, as believers give way before ridicule, subtle persecution and criticism, and the constant disparaging, especially in the media, of all efforts to affirm or live out gospel truths and values.

3

Heaven has always offered guidance

I call you friends, because I have made known to you everything that I have learnt from my Father. (Jn 15:15)

We might seek to respond to the hopelessness that prevails at the end of the twentieth century by asking if there is any serious alternative outlook? Is it, for example, still possible to make any kind of assertion of belief that will hold in a post-modern society, a society which has undermined all universal norms and meanings? It may be the case that this book would never have been begun without a belief that there was an alternative stemming from a spiritual or religious view of life, but this does not mean that such matters are easy to write about. All the evidence from current public discussion of religion would seem to suggest that the effort is fruitless. It seems to lead only to greater agnosticism. Where then does religious thinking stand? Is it possible to find solace or direction in any of the religious beliefs that have marked human history? Or has the time come to jettison the fundamentally Christian tenets of Western civilisation as mere ballast that is now simply helping the vessel to go down?

This chapter is necessarily a difficult one, difficult to write and difficult no doubt for some readers to receive, let alone accept. It makes strong claims for the Catholic Church and its teaching, but it seeks to do so reasonably rather than polemically. The strength of the prophecy currently sweeping through the Catholic Church depends upon these claims, however, for the authenticity of prophecy depends upon the faithfulness of the prophet. In any case, the argument is that the moral and spiritual state of the world is so grave that the remedy is bound to be radical, counter-cultural and therefore unwelcome to most people, at least initially. It is in fact easy to see how any Christian statement is handicapped in a secular world. The language of Christianity is either unfamiliar to those who have been raised outside of any religious tradition, or resented by many for whom it carries disagreeable historical overtones and associations. For similar reasons, the content of the message is obscured. Or those who speak for Christianity may lack the persuasive powers of carriers of other messages. Christian disunity may act to discredit the particular version of the message that is being offered. Or alternatives may simply seem more plausible, whether they are the immediate allurements of materialistic living, the more humanly flattering New Age creeds, or the more intellectually appealing arguments of a rational-scientific approach to reality.

When some Catholics say they do not want to be told what to think by the Church they may not simply be commenting on Church style but claiming the right to hold theological opinions at variance with Church teaching. Against this Christian relativism, or a widely espoused doctrinal pluralism, is the Catholic Church's claim that its teaching is based on Revelation, that is the truth revealed deliberately and definitively by God as the means of human salvation. The Catholic Church also claims that it teaches all that it is necessary to know to obtain salvation. This does not mean that Catholics are all to be saved, or that they are better than anyone else, or that others will not be saved, but that God intended the Catholic Church to be the principal repository of truth in the fullness of his self-revelation to humanity. I believe that orthodox Catholics have a consistent and coherent position, but one which they hold by reasoned faith and not by limiting their beliefs to empirical or scientific evidence. When Jesus warned his disciples to have 'nothing to do with the leaven of the Pharisees and Sadducees ' (Mt 16:9) he was evidently speaking of the need to discern false arguments and to confront them with the truths of faith.

To claim that Christianity is a *revealed* religion means that its adherents believe that the truths of their faith are not the work of human imagination, still less of feeling or preference, but were deliberately revealed to humanity by God. The first written account of this Revelation is in the Scriptures, both Old and New Testaments. The Old Testament records Israel's experience of God, through its history, its religious traditions and the teachings of its prophets. For Christians, the Old Testament also contains innumerable prophecies and foreshadowings of the fuller Revelation to be brought by Jesus Christ. The New Testament is the record of the moral and spiritual guidance given by Jesus to the Church and to all who are guided by it, that is the friends to whom he has told everything he learnt from the Father. This is not a mere philosophy; it is God's law, but a law that does not have any immediate or discernible sanctions. It relies upon individuals being ready, through conscience and conviction, to accept and follow the teaching. But the principle is very clear: it is the principle of love, for God and neighbour, and of treating others as we would wish to be treated ourselves.[12]

These teachings are received in several ways. Prayerful reading of Scripture is the most commonly accepted way amongst Christians, but for Catholics the apostolic tradition and authority of the Church transmitting the teachings of Jesus Christ are no less important for the knowledge of divine truth. The example of holiness given by the saints is another way, but always subject to Church discernment and authority. The greatest of the saints is the Blessed Virgin Mary and, in Catholic eyes, she has had a hugely significant role in Christian evangelisation, not only by her example as the mother of Jesus and his close associate throughout his life on earth, but also through her many apparitions and the messages of teaching and encouragement that she has given through human intermediaries over the centuries. The guidance offered to humanity, not just to Christians, whether by Scripture, the Church, the saints, or contemporary prophetic messages, is essentially an incitement to personal and spiritual renewal. It is a call to return to the values of love, holiness, peace, joy and hope that were taught by Jesus and reflected in his life.

Revelation through Scripture and the Church

Guard what has been entrusted to you. (1 Tm 6:20)

After my reconversion to faith I interested myself in scriptural and spiritual writings as part of my search to consolidate my belief. However, this was never a purely intellectual quest. The discovery I was led to of the richness of Scripture was extremely important to me, and I know that there is no substitute for this element of the Christian life. My sense of Scripture only really came alive after a biblical retreat I made in the Holy Land in 1987, in which I was able to spend time at Bible sites in prayer and study. From that experience I have a graphic sense of the Bible that lifts it from the page, and I am enthusiastic about initiatives that bring the Scriptures more into people's lives. Many Catholics, largely owing to their other practices of prayer and worship, have in the past had a very limited awareness of this spiritual treasure. This situation, however, is now beginning to change, no doubt in part as one of the fruits of Christian ecumenism.

The original Revelation in the Old Testament was confirmed by Jesus Christ, the Son of God who became man to bring the 'good news' or Gospel, and to found a special community, the Church, to unite all those who accepted his teaching, and especially his promise of eternal life. This Church has not only a human but also a mystical character. This means that it is always imperfectly realised in human terms, while at the same time it is infinitely more than it appears in its institutional form. For this reason the Church, being the Body of Christ through the incarnation, and thus the carrier of the divinely revealed truth, stands essentially outside social and political structures. The Catholic Church has always recognised Scripture and tradition as making up 'a single sacred deposit of the Word of God' (*Dei Verbum*, para 10). There was no canon of Scripture until the Church decided what it should contain, and therefore the Church has from the beginning been the interpreter of the Word of God whether in its written form or in the form of 'Tradition' (*Dei Verbum*, para 10). It is for this reason that Catholics do not accept the exclusiveness of the Evangelical doctrine of *sola scriptura*, that is, the Revelation of the faith from Scripture alone. In practical terms it can be seen from history that this doctrine has led to continuous divisions in the churches, taking them far away from what Jesus desired when he prayed that all would be one.

In common with other Christians, and indeed with the Jewish faith as far as the Old Testament is concerned, the Catholic Church teaches the inerrancy of Scripture. However, Catholics also accept sacred tradition as interpreted by the teaching authority, or Magisterium, of the Catholic Church, particularly as vested in the Bishop of Rome when officially teaching on matters of faith and morals, as free from error, that is, infallible. In accepting that the truth has been revealed by God through Scripture and tradition, Catholics do not imply that the truths of apostolic teaching can be extended. The teachings of the Church since the end of the apostolic times are not concerned with new truths, but with the fuller understanding of the deposit of faith, that is, everything entrusted to the Church by God.[13]

It is by reference to Scripture and tradition that the Holy Spirit guides the Church. This does not mean that there are not other ways to approach the truth, such as private enlightenment by God, the common view of the faithful (*sensus fidelium*), the development of doctrine by scholars, personal conscience and reflection on the faith. The content of Revelation broadly encompasses the divine law, the promise of salvation for the just, the nature of God and his works, and the special character and mission of Jesus, the incarnate God. Underlying everything is the belief that there is a God who made humankind, and who loves it and desires its eternal well-being. This said, there are certain spiritual and doctrinal truths that need to be stated and explained if the guidance given by the Catholic Church is to be better understood.

Spiritual and doctrinal truths

> *If you make my word your home you will indeed be my disciples, you will learn the truth, and the truth will make you free.*
> (Jn 8:31–32)

People are still asking Pontius Pilate's ironical question: 'Truth, what is that?' (Jn 18:38). In essence, they are supposing that there is no truth, and that all religions are therefore of equivalent value, or indeed of no value. This sceptical attitude can express itself in a variety of ways. Some maintain that all religions are necessarily involved in an ongoing search, and the fact that Jesus claimed to be the Truth cannot be a part of the argument for Christianity. His truth, they would say, must be assessed from the outside as with any other belief system, or simply left to the individual's free choice. Others account for religions as human inventions corresponding only to commonly experienced internal drives and instincts, or to external political interests.

In centuries past the Christian Church was divided by succeeding waves of disputes over matters of order, doctrine and practice, as well as by politically motivated struggles, until the time came when the Church split into parts, and these parts then split further. The process of the Reformation has thus continued, but now the Christian body shows new fissures. There are tendencies to ecumenism and to schism occurring at the same time within and across the churches, so that it appears likely that there will be further divisions cutting across denominations, and very probably new alignments. The polarisation of traditional and progressive theologies has constituted a general movement in many ways not unlike the original Reformation, and it is fundamental enough to threaten a 'new Reformation' in the Christian Church, including the reputedly cohesive and conservative Catholic Church.

Public commentators, even many claiming a religious viewpoint, seem to be waiting to pounce on anyone who expresses an attitude of obedience or submission to a Supreme Being (cf. Cupitt, 1994). They are appalled at the notion that they should submit, and they choose rather to speak of the God within, the God who is with us in the depths of our misery and pain. They want to struggle more than they want to be at peace. They want to win more than they want to share. They would rather present themselves as right in their subjectivity, though that has no way of being validated, than as wrong, repentant and hopeful for forgiveness. It is not new that alternatives to older beliefs are held up as more attractive, more relevant to contemporary needs, and more credible. However,

Contentious issues within the Catholic Church

- dissent among theologians in relation to the authority of Church teaching
- open criticism and even ridiculing of Church leaders
- syncretism of Christianity and Marxist theories
- anxiety among Church leaders about being seen publicly to condemn moral and other positions that are at odds with the teaching of the Church Magisterium
- a widespread notion that the individual conscience can ignore the Church
- New Age theories being incorporated into Christian faith
- a loss of a spiritual sense of direction by the young even in Christian families
- a rationalising of divine truths by intellectuals within the Church
- a widespread loss of belief in the transcendent and the miraculous
- challenge to basic doctrines such as the Eucharist, the Virgin birth, and the resurrection
- rejection of the unique authority of the See of Peter within the Church
- refusal to honour Mary as Mother of God and of the Church

this spirit of criticism and revision is so strong that it threatens Christian Revelation itself. There is growing awareness of a form of religious persecution in the West that bears more on traditional Christian believers than on any others. Christians are often accused of holding to impossible beliefs and rules, even though their moral arguments and spiritual values are given little public consideration. The media virtually censor their viewpoint by ignoring it or treating it with the scorn of political correctness. Western religious persecution is quite different from that practised until recently under Communist regimes of the East, but it is no less powerful. When religious beliefs are attacked or ridiculed, believers are often shamed into concealing what they think, or into withholding their support for those who are being targeted.

The Catholic Church's claim to the 'splendour of truth' (John Paul II, 1993) can only be tested by direct involvement, not by mere observation or study, because people cannot be convinced by rational argument when human pride, insecurity, fear, or prejudice are invading the discussion. It is only in prayer that understanding can dawn. Does this not mean that outsiders can never understand until they come to the point of praying for understanding? In the end, there cannot be any alternative to the grace of God coming like a whirlwind to disturb the 'rational' but, in fact, emotionally charged workings of the mind. Religious believers have had to undergo the strictures of rationalism to such a degree that it is humanly surprising that they have not all ended up as atheists. The only possible reason for this is that there are ways to knowledge, and indeed to truth, that are more trustworthy than the self-sufficient intellect. Heart and soul have as much to do with the matter as does the mind.

But how can people make any kind of appraisal of the teaching of the Christian churches if their minds are closed by doubt or mistrust, if, for example, they are not ready to listen to what Catholics actually say and believe about Jesus, about faith, and how they actually perceive the Church, the Papacy, the Virgin Mary, or the moral issues of the day? The attitude of contempt so often expressed in the media for the Church's teaching of moral absolutes as in the *Catechism of the Catholic Church* (CCC), or in the papal encyclicals *Veritatis Splendor* and *Evangelium Vitae*, are only comprehensible if those concerned have an unspiritual viewpoint. Although such critics do not very often strive to understand the basis for the Catholic position, it would clarify matters if they could be persuaded to respond to the following questions:

> Do you believe in a personal God? If not, then it is necessary to take into account that Christianity does.
>
> What do you believe about Jesus, assuming that you do not actually contend that he never existed? Was he simply a good man, was he an impostor, was he deluded, or was he divine, given that he claimed to be the Son of God and the saviour of humanity?

> What grounds do you have for hope in life? Is there anything you can point to that is as coherent as the Gospel, assuming you are not speaking in ignorance of the Gospel?
>
> Do you pray? Why should a loving God not answer a prayer for faith? Are you willing to pray for spiritual insight, and if not, why not?

The failure of justice and fairness in religious controversy is not necessarily due to a lack of integrity in the individuals concerned. Sheer indifference that stems from the atheism or practical atheism of the contemporary world is, in its effects, as much a problem as deliberate wrongdoing. However, much more serious is the venomous and wholly negative influence for evil of the powers at work seeking to confuse believers and unbelievers alike and to obscure the truth. Neglect of attention to the spiritual dimension of life could be the result of indifference or it could come from malign intent. Mockery of religious attitudes can be mere unkindness or it can be intended to undermine and destroy. Self-righteous attitudes of humanist concern can be misconceptions or they can be postures calculatedly aimed to deceive by their assumed respectability.

There is a spiritual battle in progress that is not merely of earthly dimensions. God has allowed this opposition because he wishes to give human beings the dignity of freely choosing their commitment. We are urged to choose life, which is to say the goodness, truth and love of God's being and creation, but we are free to choose death, which is turning our backs on God and everything that leads to the truth. The battle is within every heart and throughout the human world, as well as in the realm of the spirits. The source of evil in the spiritual world is the rebellion of Satan and his angels, and our own rebellion as human beings is provoked by the false hopes and desires of the original rebels who still seek to seduce us. Engaging in this battle to find our way to God the Father is the agenda of each human life, whether or not this is consciously realised. This spiritual warfare can manifest itself within the Church, when Christian people disgrace themselves or their offices in such a way as to cause public scandal that undermines trust and faith in the community as a whole. Those who promote their own version of the faith in the place of valid doctrine, or who rebel against Church authority or deliberately attack the Church and what it stands for, are even more clearly enlisted in another cause.[14]

The key to discernment of good and evil must always be the signs of love and humility. Where these are present there can be confidence that the truth is not far away. Once these are banished, and replaced by bitterness and pride, there can be little truth. To discern and hold to the truth requires a high degree of faith where the discussion is about making the Church part of a democratic society in relation to such contested moral issues as contraception, divorce, abortion, homosexuality, biomedical experiments, euthanasia, premarital sex or, in contrast, such spiritual values as sacrifice, penance, or belief and hope in a loving God. In its human weakness the Church is fearful of becoming irrelevant and useless, or misled by the spirit of pride and disobedience. But the Church has lasted two thousand years, and it is not going to become irrelevant in a single lifetime, even if it seems at times like the climax of a spiritual battle between the forces of light and darkness. Rebels are moved by temptation to evil, not merely by pragmatic solutions. Therefore their determination to extinguish the truth is extremely strong. It is for this reason that Christians are called by the Gospel to remain true, without any compromise, false compassion or toleration of evil.

By any reasonable standards of enquiry, therefore, anyone adopting a 'progressive' stance within the Church is obliged to be self-critical, and must surely take account of the existence of a revealed truth, of a century at least of prophetic papal teaching warning of the social disruptions of our time, of the historical centrality of Jesus incarnate as a sign of contradiction for the world, and therefore of the need for Christians to accept his life and person as normative in appraising human culture, and, finally, of the need to be able to explore the spiritual in a non-rationalistic manner, that is without placing our trust wholly, or even essentially in the human intellect. The very concept of truth is a difficult problem for the modern world. Absolutes, such as a final truth, a definitive proof, an infallible guide, or their implications in the indissolubility of marriage, the sacredness of life under all circumstances, the possibilities of eternal life and eternal damnation, are resisted, and largely refused. The Catholic Church, however, asserts such absolutes, based on Scripture and upon the tradition of Church teaching inherited from Christ and the apostles. Such teachings are accepted as the will of God, not through mere human submission by believers to the Church. They are matters of faith, or the full acceptance of Jesus Christ as the way, the truth and the life, and cannot be subject to revision. [15]

Religious pluralism has always existed, because truth and the knowledge of it are two different things. The history of the Church has constantly involved negotiations about doctrine. However, once a decision was reached it was the role of the Church to conclude matters through a general council or through a papal pronouncement. Meanwhile heresies developed, sometimes gained adherents, even led to schisms, and sometimes faded away, often to reappear in another age. Throughout, however, the Church endured as the faithful witness. In our time the situation seems to have changed. Now the very idea of truth is so widely rejected that anyone affirming the inerrancy of Scripture, the doctrinal truths of the Creed, and the moral injunctions of the Old and New Testaments, has to be prepared to be called a fundamentalist, that is, a person who is regarded as having a self-evidently mistaken belief in an absolute. However, given the Catholic teaching that the truth subsists most fully in the Catholic Church, fidelity to the Church is incompatible with the moral relativism of the present time and the doctrinal relativism of many claiming to be Christians. The very confidence with which Catholics hold to their Church despite its human failings is often a cause of reproach from others. Personally, I have never felt worried by the often virulent anti-Catholicism I have encountered. I have taken it as evidence that there is an ongoing spiritual battle, one between forces of light and darkness, not one between groups of varying shades of grey.[16] If we make God's truth our home it will set us free, we have been told.

If we ask what are the defining truths of Catholicism, there is a way of formulating them which to a large degree underlies this book. It is summed up in the doctrines of Jesus' sacrifice, the unity of the Church as Christ's body under the Bishop of Rome, and the understanding of Mary's role in our redemption. One inspiring writer renders this as: the Eucharist, Mary and Peter (Philippe, 1994, pp. 306–07). Christians receive their Christian life through the cross of sacrifice, a spiritual birth at which Mary is present. They are nourished by the Eucharist, and they are guided by Peter, to whom Jesus said 'Look after my sheep' (Jn 21:16). In fact, however, many Christians, and even Catholics understate these orthodox beliefs and the apostolic tradition of the Church in the interests of ecumenism. They seem more at ease explaining the Mass as a celebratory meal than as the everlasting sacrifice of Calvary. The Blessed Virgin Mary is often set on one side; her apparitions, her messages and her cult are ignored or downplayed by many Catholic thinkers and teachers who favour political and social interpretations of the Gospel. And the teaching authority of the Pope is challenged all over the world, including by some Church leaders, most notably in the Americas.[17]

The Eucharist

> *I am the bread of life. He who comes to me will never be hungry; he who believes in me will never thirst.* (Jn 6:35)

A key belief of the Catholic tradition acknowledges the Eucharist as the realisation of the Church's identity and unity. Jesus left the Eucharist as a memorial and as the means to sustaining the Christian community on its journey. The Catholic belief in the real presence of Christ in the Eucharist is the essential key to the meaning of the incarnation, crucifixion and resurrection of Jesus. This understanding had always been there in the doctrine I was taught as a child, but it was only in my mid-forties that I fully accepted it, when I realised that when Jesus said: 'Know that I am with you always; yes, to the end of time' (Mt 28:20), he meant it in a very literal sense. Under the appearance of the sheer ordinariness of church worship, centred around the offering of the bread and wine by the priest, there is an awesome cosmic reality, perhaps best expressed in the familiar words of Gerard Manley Hopkins' translation of St Thomas Aquinas' hymn:

> Godhead here in hiding whom I do adore
> masked by these bare shadows, shape and nothing more.

Above all, Christians believe that Jesus Christ, the divine Son of God, became man in order to make atonement to the Father, thus ensuring the salvation of those who accepted God's mercy. For Catholics, the daily liturgy of the Church, the celebration of the Mass, is the eternal sacrifice of the cross, by which Jesus redeemed those of all religions and none from the effects of sin and death by the sacrifice of his life on the cross. By participating in the Mass, in spirit and physically through Holy Communion, the people are joined with Jesus Christ and benefit from his sacrifice. The Mass is not a dramatic rendering or symbol, but the reality of Christ's self-offering presented on the altar in accordance with his specific instruction: 'Do this as a memorial of me' (Lk 22:19).

The Mass is a mystery in two senses. Firstly, without participation in the Mass it is impossible to comprehend what is signified by it, since no words can convey what is essentially an act of worship. And secondly, even to believers the Mass always remains a mystery because they are unable fully to understand how it is that Christ is present in the offering of his sacrifice on Calvary, when all they see is an assembly of people gathered around a priest following set prayers in a ritual that has taken the same form for nearly two thousand years. However, there is no doubt that the first kind of mystery at least can be got over, in that people do come to an appreciation of the centrality of the Mass to the whole activity of Christian worship, so that eventually it can become for them the core activity of their lives.

The Eucharist is the viaticum, the bread of life, the spiritual food left for believers. The Mass is the mutual offering of the people to God, and of God to the people in Christ, and therefore a sharing in the cross and in the resurrection of Jesus. The act of faith that this involves opens believers to God's promises, in an attitude that is the complete opposite of attention to the world's empty promises. The Mass is the supreme act of intercession of Jesus, with which believers associate themselves for their own sanctification and for the salvation of the world. It is thus the expression of all that is meaningful and purposeful about human existence: who we are, how we are to live, where we are going, how we will get there, how we can relate to the world, to time and eternity, the importance of our own part in things, the link we have to the divine, and the working out of what God wishes for all those he has created.

Mary's role in human salvation

> *Seeing his mother and the disciple he loved standing near her, Jesus said to his mother, 'Woman, this is your son'. Then to the disciple he said, 'This is your mother'.* (Jn 19:26)

Mary had borne the heat of the day, from the beginning in Nazareth, when the angel came to her, through the time of the crucifixion, when she stood at the foot of the cross, through the long years when she was the Mother of the nascent Church, but was separated from her Son, until the time when she was assumed into heaven at the end of her earthly life. Mary's womb was home to the God-man. Many writers speak of Mary as if she was just so humble that the Lord could have his way with her, and she was nothing. In one sense this is true, because all are created from nothing, and come to be only through God's will. However, there is no doubt that God honours Mary to an astonishing degree. He asks her through the angel to be the mother of the Redeemer. He does not treat her as a mere receptacle or robot. Then Jesus invites her at the foot of the cross to become the spiritual mother of all humanity: 'Woman, this is your son'. So while it is true that Mary is humble, she is also someone of immense dignity, and this is now recognised in her position as Queen of Heaven, crowned with twelve stars (Rv 12:1). The Mother of God deserves from humanity the same honour that is given to her by Jesus. To deny her privileges is to ignore the evidence of the Gospel, and to accept the Gospel is to honour Mary above all created beings. This is what Jesus did, and what he wishes everyone to do.

The understanding of Mary in the Christian life, while it starts with the Gospels and a couple of other New Testament references, has been one of the areas that have most shown a development of doctrine in the Church. After all, four of the very small number of infallible dogmas that have ever been proclaimed concern Mary, namely the divine Motherhood, the Perpetual Virginity, the Immaculate Conception and the Assumption. Far from being an area in which the Catholic Church can make concessions to other Christian viewpoints, it is likely that on the subject of Mary there is further doctrinal development to come. The Second Vatican Council made this clear, in the Dogmatic Constitution on the Church, where the Council Fathers say that they did not 'wish to decide those questions which have not yet been fully illuminated by the work of theologians' (*Lumen Gentium*, para 54). What this suggests is that further doctrinal development is to be anticipated. There are a number of themes with such potential that are merely mentioned in *Lumen Gentium*, with no position taken, such as Mary's role as mother to us in the order of grace (para 61), or as Mediatrix (62), and as 'cooperating in the work of human salvation' (para 56). The document also refers to 'the union of the Mother and the Son in the work of salvation' (para 57), and observes that at the cross, 'she united herself with a maternal heart to his sacrifice' (para 58).

We know Mary as mother of the Redeemer, but in a sense she is even more than this; she is the co-redeemer. She was chosen by the Father, and allowed by him to represent the remainder of the race in participating in the life of the Redeemer, though not adding anything to the power of the redemption. She was the mother of the Son, which allowed her a key role in his life on earth, but she remains his mother in her glory, and has become mother of the Church and of all people by Christ's will. She is the spouse of the Holy Spirit, and carries his divine love and power as the fruit of her womb. Mary thus links us to the Trinity as a unique mediatrix. She does not replace Christ, but it may be that she replaces all humanity so as to become the channel for all graces that come to us from God. The understanding of Mary as mediatrix of all graces is not a dogma of the Church, but it is a widely held belief that she cannot be by-passed in the dispensation of graces because of the special place that she occupies in relation to each person of the Blessed Trinity.

The Catholic and Orthodox faiths especially give great honour to Mary. Both recognise her divine and universal maternity, her sinlessness, her perpetual virginity, her sufferings shared with the crucified saviour, and her assumption into paradise. The term 'dormition' (or 'falling asleep') of the Virgin, used by the Orthodox Church, indicates the delicacy of the understanding of what happened at the end of Mary's earthly life. Did she die, or was she taken into heaven at a particular moment of her development in God's grace? One reflection that has been made is that, just as she had drawn God's Son into her womb by her perfection and humility through the power of the Holy Spirit, so she was drawn back to him in his glory after his ascension, again by the Spirit's power.

Much of this richness of tradition is rejected by the Protestant Churches. Though some have taken a more positive view, for many the Virgin is seen as a stumbling block to Christian unity. If it be so, then there must be an explanation in the Catholic way of expressing its beliefs and devotion to her. Have Catholics not understood Mary sufficiently? Have protesters been misled by confusion about Catholic belief? Is there anything wrong with the Protestant insistence upon direct communion with the Lord, and the lesser prominence given to Mary and the saints? With the impact of Medjugorje, many Catholics are asking themselves whether they have lacked the courage to speak sufficiently powerfully about Mary, to place her mission in God's hands rather than in their own over-diplomatic ones. Whether men or women, it could be that their religious development has been too masculine, too rational, to be able to be truly humble and whole-hearted, so that they could speak of these essentially Marian virtues in their words and lives, to make Mary more truly known and valued.

As regards the place of the Virgin Mary in the spiritual lives of believers, this is an area where Catholics turn to the saints for inspiration, and although Vatican II stressed the need to avoid devotional excesses, this did not stop the then Pope from writing an encyclical letter some years later on this subject. Pope Paul VI includes a powerful exhortation to recognise the theological value of devotion to Mary.

> Contemplated in the episodes of the Gospels and in the reality which she already possesses in the City of God, the Blessed Virgin Mary offers a calm vision and a reassuring word to modern man, torn as he often is between anguish and hope, defeated by the sense of his own limitations and assailed by limitless aspirations, troubled in his mind and divided in his heart, uncertain before the riddle of death, oppressed by loneliness while yearning for fellowship, a prey to boredom and disgust. She shows forth the victory of hope over anguish, of fellowship over solitude, of peace over anxiety, of joy and beauty over boredom and disgust, of eternal visions over earthly ones, of life over death. (*Marialis Cultus*, para 57)

The doctrinal and spiritual authority of the Papacy

> *You are Peter, and on this rock I will build my Church. And the gates of the underworld can never hold out against it.*
> (Mt 16:18)

What reply can be made to those, Christians or others, who attack the Catholic Church, criticising the Pope's teaching, assailing 'the Vatican' for its reactionary influence, and supporting bishops who have opposed the teaching authority of the Church in the name of justice and freedom, and a demand for democratic authority that is claimed to have been legitimated by Vatican II? What justification is there for giving loyalty to the Pope, for believing in the teaching authority of the Church, and for affirming that the Church is not a conservative force, a patriarchal anachronism, or an outmoded interpretation of the Gospel, but rather the body of Christ, the spiritual mother of all who live, and the way to peace on earth and to eternal life?

From the outside, the Catholic Church appears to be a socially and politically ordered institution governed by an absolute ruler. From within, however, the primary reality of the Church is as the mystical body of Christ, the ark of salvation, essentially not a human institution at all, but one ordained by Jesus Christ to carry on the ministry that he began while on earth: the saving of souls for eternal life. The image of the ark is a key one, because the Church travels, rescues, carries, and delivers. Every vessel needs a helmsman, and the helmsman of the Church is the Pope, the one charged on earth with steering the Church. He acts for the captain who is the source of all authority. In other more traditional words, the Pope is the Vicar of Christ on earth. All authority was given to Peter when Jesus ended his earthly life. It is against the Church led by Peter that 'the gates of the underworld can never hold out' (Mt 16: 18). The authority of the Papacy has undoubtedly been abused at times over the centuries, but its doctrinal and spiritual dimensions have endured, and indeed are more vital today than they have ever been, at a time when civil society has lost any moral consistency or spiritual sense of direction.

Recent papal encyclicals and other writings, such as the statement on women priests, and the *Catechism of the Catholic Church*, have made a massive restatement of the unchanging moral and doctrinal teaching of the Church, which is there for Christians to accept or reject in conscience. But they are all of a piece. Catholics at least can no longer pick and mix, as some have thought Vatican II gave them licence to do. There is no set of people who own the Church and who can presume to barely tolerate the Pope coming onto their territory. Only those recognised by God, and not a human elite or majority viewpoint, have authority. The protestantisation of the Catholic Church has been checked. Those who prefer to see the Reformation continue can make their choice of affiliation among the existing Christian denominations, or they can begin a new foundation. Those Catholics who have wanted a clear sign from the Holy Spirit can be at peace in the confidence that they have seen it in the beginnings of spiritual renewal in the Church.

In essence, the issue is about whether or not the Church has the right and the duty to insist upon orthodoxy in its teaching. In its own self-understanding it is of the nature of the Catholic Church that it does not have to follow a secular ethic or democratic political process, because of its divine institution. Secular models are not of relevance in matters of doctrine and morals. Even if there is a cultural aspect to the Church that means that it must communicate within a cultural context, it still functions with the authority of Christ himself, exactly as when he spoke in the Sermon on the Mount. Yet despite the widely held fears about society not being able to regulate its own behaviour, the Church is resented when it brings the authority of the Gospels into its teaching, as if it cannot be accepted that we can only reach our fulfilment by following the path God intended for us. This would imply that we should have an attitude of humility, of obedience, and not imagine that we can invent our own original view of morality. Human creativity of course exists, but it can only be fundamentally fruitful if it is in line with that of the Creator.

Since the Church is not primarily a social or a political organisation, to treat it as such is a misapprehension. Historically, however, this has constantly been practised, both from within by clergy especially, and from without by civil rulers. Women who demand 'rights' in the Church today have likewise mistaken the kind of organisation it is and the kind of commitment the Lord asks of his disciples. They have also perhaps underestimated their own special charism in the Church as women. They have identified certain attributes of male careers and experience in the secular world as being ultimately desirable in the Church, and thus they struggle to be 'equal' to men, in the sense of having these attributes in the Church. This will denature the Church, just as the building of careers and the search for power in the Church by men denatures the Church. Both men and women can better be fulfilled in their own natures and vocations by being faithful to the gospel injunction to give priority to seeking the Kingdom of God. The claims of radical feminist Catholics are doubly suspect because not only do they seek to change the nature of the Church into a secular form, but they brush aside men, lay men, as having no significance. In other words they compare themselves to priests and bishops, not to lay men. They do not seek common cause with lay men to ensure that the lay voice is heard in the Church, not as of right but for the building of the Kingdom. These polemics can only impede the apostolic activity of the Church. It would be far better to put genuinely womanly virtues to work for the Kingdom. The Church needs to change, but only to become more loving, more caring, more nurturing and more spiritual.

Despite a virtually worldwide media campaign treating the present Pope as a reactionary despot, it is noteworthy that he has never responded in kind, but instead seeks to guide people to spiritual improvement and to hope. However, he has not hesitated to speak of a grave crisis of faith, to reject the disunity of dissident theologians, and to identify clearly those tendencies that destroy the coherence of the Catholic vision and which could lead people away from the truth (John Paul II, 1993 and 1994). He uses Scripture to indicate how such rebellions are ever-recurring features of humanity's relationship with God, caused by the presence of sin and the influence of Satan who is the father of lies and who was the first to reject God. The dissent and rebellion referred to are often camouflaged. They are justified in the name of freedom, justice, equality, human rights, civilisation, personal autonomy, self-esteem, as well as by the epithets of liberal, progressive, or democratic. In fact the claims made are almost overwhelming. Who would want to be thought to oppose such self-evidently 'good' values? It is precisely the aim of the encyclical letter, *Veritatis Splendor,* to show up the speciousness of the thinking that attempts to impose itself, without having any other basis than popular assent. This is why John Paul II warns of the short step from liberalism to totalitarianism. Far more justified is the position that all values are to be calibrated with human reason, but must find their foundation in the independently existing Absolute of the Divinity and the sure teaching revealed by Scripture and by Christ, and preserved in the teaching of the Church.

Those who say that the Pope has no right to tell them what to think are free to reject his authority. He is not in fact telling them what to think. If people feel in their hearts that they should listen, then they should listen. Otherwise he has no authority over them, and they have no cause to feel aggrieved. It can only be their own consciences speaking to them if they do feel aggrieved. But there are also Catholics who presume to speak in the name of their co-religionaries in rejecting the Pope's teaching. These are forced to place themselves above the Pope to maintain that his teaching is out of order. Where does their authority stem from, and how can they justify any confidence in what they say? Isn't the very fact of these attacks, for example those of Hans Küng, the dissenting German theologian, good grounds for recognising the necessity of Church authority?

Pope John Paul II is credited by many, including Mikhail Gorbachev, as making a key contribution to the fall of Communism in Eastern Europe and the Soviet Union. However, the acclaim he might otherwise receive for this is muted because he is seen as taking a position on moral issues which is out of line with progressive modern thinking. This state of alienation, which John Paul II calls the 'culture of death', is unlikely to be modified in his lifetime. He will never himself receive the appreciation due to him, but there is little doubt that history will recognise him as having been a unique force for good, both moral and political, during his pontificate. A slight foretaste of this appeared in France in 1996, when the Press almost universally forecast popular rejection of Pope John Paul on the occasion of his visit to celebrate the fifteen hundredth anniversary of the baptism of King Clovis. It was said that the streets would be filled with protesters at his interference in the affairs of a secular state. As it turned out the opposite happened. Very few protesters materialised. Large crowds of Catholic faithful came to the Reims airfield for the ceremony, and the media received a severe shock. The Papacy once more revealed that its influence has little to do with conventional public relations.

The primacy of faith

> *If your lips confess that Jesus is Lord and if you believe in your heart that God raised him from the dead, then you will be saved.* (Rm 10:9)

The Eucharist, Mary and Peter, then, are cardinal elements of Catholic faith, and these have a higher value than human rationality because the confession of faith is the condition of salvation. The 'Sea of Faith' Anglicans and their sympathisers, on the other hand, have so completely espoused a rationalist reinterpretation of faith that they have evacuated all Revelation, all transcendence (Cupitt, 1984). Catholic conviction lies rather with the preservation of these truths and yet the ongoing renewal of the Church, its faith, and its religious culture, by substituting wisdom for rationalism, obedience for arrogance, unity for individualism, hope for stoicism, the heart for the head, and peace for division. In fact, the ancient tradition remains unbroken. The Church still exists as the guardian of the revealed truth, and as the source of authority for interpretation of Scripture and the teaching of faith and morals. Believers are bound by obedience, in living out a conscious Christian life, not in self-assertion and protest against the Church's divine institution, but in humility, discernment and a constant effort to inform their personal conscience.[19]

Faith is the distinctive starting-point, because everything changes according to whether someone believes in God. If there is no God we are on our own, trapped in ourselves, however nobly disguised. Even if we claim belief in God we still run the risk of deceiving ourselves and pursuing our own interests and self-exaltation instead. So it is not simply believing in God that counts, but being committed to knowing, loving, honouring and obeying him. That is where faith comes in at a higher level than simple belief. Faith is in the things unseen, but faith also expects something of God, that he will hold good to his promises, and that he has a plan for each person's existence. What distinguishes the Christian from the secularist is faith, the belief in another reality hidden by a veil from human eyes and minds. In their Creed, Christians say they believe in God and in life everlasting. It is these two things that are essential. That is, they believe that they are created by a God who has a plan that includes them, by which they become his adopted sons and daughters. Nothing else matters, since his plan is far greater than anything human intelligence can conceive. It follows, in the logic of faith, that human plans are worthless beside his. If we prefer our own projects to his, we make them into idols, denying him in order to exalt ourselves or what our minds have conceived. God calls us to be obedient, not to humiliate us, but to take us along the path of real, objective truth about his creation. And where does that path lead? To everlasting life in heaven with God.

Our destiny is to be gathered up into God, into his

Trinitarian life, and this is the great mystery of Christianity which places it before all other beliefs. We have been initiated into the divine life by the revelation through Jesus of the existence of the Blessed Trinity. We are in need of purification, but our eternal life in the Spirit has already begun, and in an embryonic sense we are already experiencing that Trinitarian life, just as the fetus is already experiencing human life while still in the womb. The fetus in the womb may in fact be the best analogy we have to our own existence before our death and resurrection to the life of paradise. This teaching about the Holy Trinity is very difficult to comprehend, and if it is to move us we must continually reflect on our relationship to the Trinity as taught in the Scriptures: we are sons of the Father, brothers and co-heirs with Christ, and temples of the Spirit. We receive the Holy Spirit, the living water of grace and love, from the pierced heart of Jesus crucified, according to the will of the Father.

Heaven has always offered guidance, in the sense that there is no such thing as spiritual self-reliance. God's revelation of himself to humanity is his gift, not a human achievement, since God is infinitely more than human powers of thought or imagination could ever discern. Many have hoped that it would be possible to derive a wisdom from religion that would bring worldly advantages, but such hopes have usually been short-lived. The only adequate response to the Gospel is by faith, hope and love, the way lived most radically by Jesus, Mary and the saints. We can call this radical way 'mystical', because it pierces the veil that separates earthly and heavenly realities. It always sees the reality beyond, and therefore seeks God's Kingdom rather than earthly advantage as an absolute principle, if necessary preferring death to disloyalty to God's precepts. It is therefore not some vague release or happiness that is expected, but the working out of God's deliberate intentions and promises to all humanity.

Divine guidance is needed if people are to realise the truth of their condition and the change of life that is needed if they are to be united with God in eternity. The fruits of this guidance are especially seen in the lives of saints and martyrs who have been able to give their lives as witnesses to what they knew by the grace of faith to be the truth. The fact that God can reach everyone through the inner voice of their own spirit and conscience does not mean that more specific external guidelines, such as those given by the Church, can be casually disregarded. This work therefore aims to highlight the main pillars of the needed response: a return to the Scripture-based revelation of truth, and a journey in faith and morality guided by the Church, and by the discernment of ordinary Christians of all denominations, including those who have received direct inspirations or prophecies from God and through the Blessed Virgin Mary. This divine guidance urges everyone, whether they are believers or not, to a total spiritual renewal of their lives.

4

Prophecy in the Church

Prophets and prophecy

No more does the Lord Yahweh do anything without revealing his plans to his servants the prophets. (Am 3:7)

Whether widely accepted or not, there have always been prophets in the Judeo-Christian world from the earliest biblical times until today. They were plentiful among the ancient Hebrews, as they drew people's attention to their misdeeds and called them to reform. One of the opening scenes of the Gospels features John the Baptist's prophetic warning to 'flee from the retribution that is coming ' (Mt 3:8), and we might see Jesus as the greatest of the prophets were this role not overshadowed by the fact of his divine incarnation. Subsequently, the Virgin Mary has become the most prominent heavenly messenger through her apparitions and warning messages over the centuries, though these have never been so frequent nor with such a note of urgency as at the present time.

Prophecy is a gift of the Holy Spirit. Such gifts have always been recognised by the Church, and are clearly prized by St Paul:

> You must want love more than anything else, but still hope for the spiritual gifts as well, especially prophecy ... the man who prophesies does so for the benefit of the community.
> (1 Co 14:1–5)

The gifts of the Holy Spirit are for the building of the Church and for its unity. But to be effective these gifts must be used in obedience to the authority of the Church. There is no doubt that it is often an uphill struggle for a person with a prophetic message to be heard in the Church, since of its nature prophecy is challenging and normally constitutes a demand for change. However, authentic gifts will sooner or later be accepted, and will serve the Church. The Church, in its turn, must discern with care whatever is proposed, to ensure that it is consonant with Church teaching, not contrary to Revelation in Scripture and Church tradition, that the mode and circumstances of its presentation are fitting to confirm its credibility and appropriateness, and that it has positive fruits in Christian spiritual formation and life.[20] Criteria of discernment must however be applied prayerfully, not mechanically, so that genuine messages from God are recognised through their good fruits, such as conversions, faith and peacefulness.

It is the same today as it was in Old Testament times. Prophets must not allow themselves to be silenced. Ezechiel tells us that whatever words the prophet hears he must speak in the name of God, regardless of whether he is listened to or not (Ezk 3: 2–11). This is the role of the prophet. It is God's business to stir the rebellious heart to repentance; the prophet simply has to speak as he hears. He must confront the mystery of unbelief in complete faith, humility, and obedience. But this is true for all believers, since they are called to pray for the conversion of those who do not yet know of God's love. And the force that should motivate them to oppose the values of the world with this unconditional love, humility, perseverance and obedience, is the awareness in faith of sorrow, of compassion, of pain at the injustice of the world with the irruption of sin which has disturbed its beauty, its harmony, its God-given nature and the whole order of creation, with God being made man and then becoming the sign that is rejected.

The Christian, like the Jew, finds in the Old Testament the prophecies of the coming of the Messiah, the Saviour King. Jesus told the disciples on the road to Emmaus that this was the main message of the Scriptures. This prophetic tradition continues into the New Testament, especially in the Gospels

The perennial character of scriptural prophecy

Amos 3:1–15 can serve as an illustration of how scriptural prophecy retains its relevance for the Church

- the prophet speaks for God in a world which daily declares its unbelief.
- the Lord's message to the House of Israel through the prophet is:
- a reproach that they have sinned even though they had been especially chosen, and a threat of punishment (v.2)
- a reference to all the signs that had been given, for the Lord does not do anything without revealing his plans to his servants the prophets (vv. 3–7)
- the identification of Israel's wrongs, the warning of destruction (vv.9–11)
- the fate of the victims and their cherished possessions (v. 12)
- the message to those who have been faithless, those who should have known how to live but have turned away and acted unjustly (v.13)
- when the chosen people offend him, the Lord is especially roused to anger, but as he never acts without making his case clear through his prophets, when he does do this his meaning takes on a universal relevance
- Old Testament prophets do not speak only to their own times
- the message of Amos is as much to the Church today as to the ancient Hebrews

and in the Acts of the Apostles. Jesus' life on earth was accompanied by a whole series of prophetic announcements. His coming was announced to Mary and to Joseph by the Archangel Gabriel, and then to the shepherds, to Simeon and to Anna, to Elizabeth, and to John the Baptist. Most of these figures were then led to prophesy themselves. Mary, in her Magnificat prayer, acknowledges both her own eternal blessing, as one who has become the Mother of God, and her confidence in the universal and everlasting character of God's forgiveness and mercy. Inspired by a dream, Joseph prophetically names his foster son Jesus, the One who saves. Simeon and Anna also proclaim the Saviour, and Elizabeth foresees the birth of Jesus and acclaims the faith shown by Mary. John the Baptist is the prophet who heralds the Lord, preparing the way before him, as all four Gospels relate. And Jesus, when he has grown to manhood, foretells his own suffering, death, resurrection from the tomb and his return to glory in heaven. He also foretells the future life of humanity, its trials, and its eternal salvation with him in his Father's Kingdom.

The New Testament gives us many examples of how the fulfilment of the earlier prophecies of the coming of the Messiah was acknowledged. In his first letter, Peter says:

> It was this salvation that the prophets were looking and searching so hard for; their prophecies were about the grace that was to come to you. The Spirit of Christ that was in them foretold the sufferings of Christ and the glories that would come after them. (1 P 1:10–11)

Prophets are regarded by St Paul as an essential part of the Church community; the prophets, along with the apostles, are the foundation of the Church (Ep 2:20), and prophecy is spoken of as a spiritual gift to be especially hoped for (1 Cor 14:1). The Acts of the Apostles names several people who are reputed as prophets, for example, Agabus, whose prediction of a famine was taken seriously by the whole Church, and in fact was fulfilled soon afterwards (Ac 11: 27–28).

In the same way today, prophets call for the purification and strengthening of the Christian faith in the world, so that a pagan culture can once more be transformed and welcome the good news of salvation. However, for many, the messenger on the mountains in Isaiah is now remote, and he is not likely to be heard by contemporary culture. Does it not therefore seem plausible that there can be other messengers, whose function it is to bring this same message today? Contemporary prophecy merely echoes the prophecies of long ago, like the watchmen whose voices echo one another's in the Judean hills. It is the same message, always the same announcement of redemption, but with different ways of reaching the ears of the deaf and the eyes of the blind. It has been the natural defence of the pagan, the agnostic or the atheist who does not want to change his or her position or lifestyle to mock anyone who claims to speak for God, but that is precisely what prophets and visionaries are called to do. The unbeliever and the messenger from God are on a collision course. When such a messenger is derided, however, he or she is mirroring the sufferings of Jesus, who was mocked with the crown of thorns although he spoke the truth, and perhaps precisely because he did so. When Heaven wants to be heard it will be heard, no matter what scorn or deafness it encounters.

For those who believe in God it should not be difficult for them to concede that he can appoint spokespersons or messengers, even where they feel uncomfortable with, or suspicious of a particular message. Did not the prophet Joel declare for Yahweh?

> I will pour out my Spirit on all mankind; your sons and daughters shall prophesy; your old men shall dream dreams, and your young men see visions. (Jl 3:1)

It should therefore not surprise believers if they see this happening, with many people in the world today claiming to have heavenly apparitions, while others are given privileged insights into God's view of the world and 'the mystery of his purpose'. This is not to imply that any claimant of heavenly messages should be accepted as authentic without the most careful discernment. Even when the Church pronounces a claimed supernatural phenomenon as worthy of belief Catholics are not obliged to believe in it. Similarly, believers can choose to heed or not to heed the warnings prophetic messengers offer. But the better course is to consider whether the message being offered is plausible or not. In so many cases it is, and Christians risk no error by following the teaching when it is simply a restatement of the Gospel adapted to current times.

The message of the prophets

> *You foolish men, so slow to believe the full message of the prophets.* (Lk 24:25)

The common theme of many contemporary prophecies is that the world is in a state of moral and spiritual crisis, that this is wholly displeasing to God, and that he urgently desires spiritual renewal everywhere. For Christian believers the truth in such messages is self-evident, whether on the basis of personal experience or from seeing the world through the media, but it is still the case that most people do not like to be told about sin, because they see this as restricting their freedom to pursue wealth, pleasure and power. Giving such messages can therefore be guaranteed to provoke squeals of protest, denials and justifications. But sin is not freedom; it is a form of enslavement, as Christians know. True freedom lies in the forgiveness of sin by God (Ep 1:7). It follows that the prophets' warnings are messages of hope not of doom, provided only that the hearers respond by turning their backs on sin. These are the points of emphasis that emerge again and again from the declarations of Heaven's messengers, and they indicate the ways in which all people are called to respond in their own lives. The most hopeful thing, however, is that Heaven is being heard by millions who are confidently taking the path of spiritual renewal in accordance with God's will and Mary's urgings. We can therefore refute attempts to dismiss contemporary prophecies as mere 'doom and gloom'. The doom and gloom belong, it is sad to say, to those who are so attached to their worldly ways that they are not prepared to change them even for the sake of the Kingdom.

Through the prophets we are constantly reminded of the ultimate level of truth that speaks directly of God and his concern for humanity and its redemption. As it was with the first coming of the Saviour so it will be with his second coming. We have the harbingers of this, but they cannot be seen by human eyes unaided, only by the light of faith and through grace. The Holy Spirit is inspiring the Church, allowing it to be guided by the Blessed Virgin Mary, and calling on all believers to become prophets for others, according to the light they have received. Prophecy is not merely messages about the forthcoming working out of God's justice, but about his vision of the world as it is, how he wants it to change, what he wants his people to do, as well as what he intends as the long-term result of his plans. Far from being a preoccupation of exclusive sects waiting on mountain tops, this is mainstream Christian theology and it is a prominent part of the lives, teachings and testament of saints and prophets in the history of the Church. The prophets are part of the community of faith, even if at times in tension with its leaders. But when we take in the full perspective of time and space we can see that the prophet is part of the people, sustained by their prayer and expressing their faith and hope.

It is an axiom for Christians to follow the Gospels, but this does not imply disregarding the messages of modern prophets, including those that stem from mystical apparitions and the inner locutions received by certain individuals, since these are often the very indicators that will point us back to the Gospel. Why should there not be a modern Amos or Isaiah? To reject such a possibility out of hand is to risk being blind and deaf to prophecy by throwing out the baby of truth with the bathwater of false prophets. If 'love sees what other people cannot see' then it should be able to see God acting through his prophets, whether in Scripture or in contemporary life, rather than being like 'foolish men, so slow to believe'. It is true that there is a genuine problem of discernment, but discernment is one thing, scepticism about timely warnings from Heaven quite another. Indeed, what we risk by neglect of God's warnings is contributing to a collapse of the faith, a 'reform' in which the very things that are essential are abandoned while the trappings of a false order are preserved.

The Old Testament prophets, as in the case of Amos, speak the truth about God's judgement for his people who are to be chastised for their unfaithfulness by exile, deprivation and humiliation. It cannot be any different today. We are now convicted of unfaithfulness, irresponsibility, laziness, and of not taking God seriously. In the messages through his prophets of today God is saying the same things. Our sins will be visited with a refining fire, for our redemption and salvation, though out of mercy more than justice. The world cannot hear this voice, or cannot credit it with any plausibility. Only what is known to reason and the senses is considered creditworthy, and so most ears are deaf. That those who read the Scriptures with devotion should take the same attitude however is the greatest betrayal. It may not be the godless ones who most need purification, for they might change in an instant if they glimpsed the eternal reality, but rather those who have been told everything they needed to know by God's messengers, and have refused to give it a hearing.

The Bible is full of warnings, often conditional, from God about actions he intended, and of accounts of those who heard them, as well as of those who did not. In fact the great figures of the Old Testament were those who heeded God's warnings and directed the people accordingly, such as Noah, Abraham, Moses, Joseph, and the prophets themselves. In New Testament times the warnings are more explicit, and accompanied by specific moral teachings and by the institution of the Church as the guardian of God's people until the end of time (Mt 28:20). In prophecy, whether in Scripture or at the present time, we find the things hoped for. In hope, we live for the realisation of God's plan known to us in faith, whether through the prophets sent to us in ancient times, in the person of Christ, or in our own time. The two terms, prophecy and hope, contain an extraordinary programme for faith. If we believe, we have the doors of eternal life opened to us and we do not have to focus our concern exclusively upon our life in this world. On the other hand, no one can afford to be indifferent to the messages of the prophets, because they tell of God's plans and of the means of their realisation - including each individual's contribution.

The vital role of the prophet is to continually recall to mind these 'heavenly things' (Col 3:2), since the Church community is always at risk of settling down into routines and assumptions which belong to everyday life. The prophet is the one who sees the wood for the trees, and who demands that everyone awakens from their earthly slumber and looks to God's word and his interests. We are encouraged by this word to wrench ourselves away from everything that holds us earthbound so that we can truly see, and this wrenching is a work of faith. There is an application here for the whole Christian life. We are to take the word of God as a promise, in faith. It is to cause us to be renewed and purified. We are to hear the message of the ancient prophets because they had the Spirit of God in them, and they prepare us to recognise and follow the Messiah, now that the whole mystery has been made plain to us by the evangelists. Contemporary prophets, too, clarify the call of God, making plain the word of God already known from Scripture, renewing our hope and purifying our souls by reference to God's work and to his plan of salvation.

Messengers have always been used (cf. Is 52; Rm 10: 15), even though God is not obliged to tell us his plans through human means, and sometimes he finds other ways. The word 'angel' means messenger, and God has sent his angels to give specific messages, most notably the message to Mary that she would bear the Son of God. None the less, there is a very important and mysterious function that God assigns to certain individuals throughout the ages. These are the authentic messengers, who do not give their own message but who speak God's words. There is nothing to mark out such people from others who invent or imagine what they say, or who are using people's good faith or gullibility to mislead them and to take advantage of them. We cannot immediately know which is the case. However, Jesus is the divine messenger, and all prophets who are genuine are his messengers. That is why, when we read the prophecies of the Old Testament, we do not need to be concerned about which particular historical circumstance the message fits. The message may well be for a specific situation, but it is also a message for each age, and for all time, because it expresses God's promises which never change, and which are always being realised, in individuals, in situations, in the world and the whole cosmos. So the messengers on the mountains that bring good news are always coming over the brow of the hill. The watchmen who raise their voices and cry out all together are always crying out at the explosion of the Lord's redemptive mercy. Sion is constantly being restored; the captives are all the time being released from their exile. This is happening in every day of our lives; it is simply a question of our having the eyes of faith to perceive it.

While it is the case that we have the problem of discerning true from false prophets, the difficulty of discernment does not justify our closing our ears to prophecy that could be true, simply because we also reason that it could be false.

> Do not stifle the utterances of the Spirit...; and yet you must scrutinise it all carefully, retaining only what is good, and rejecting all that has the look of evil about it. (1 Th 5:19)

Scripture teaches that we should judge things by their fruits, and Catholic faith also affirms that no valid prophecy can be against the teaching and beliefs of the Church, nor can it promote actions that are morally disordered. Therefore part of the matter of discernment has to do with the prophet's loyalty to the Church. The Church has not told the 'true' prophets what to say, so they are not mere conformists, but they must be willing to submit what they say in prophecy to the discernment of the Church. Anyone who proposes something to the Church and its people which demands a response of love, commitment, or sacrifice, but who does not press on with their message further than the Church allows, stays within Church obedience. Thus, the German priest announcing plans to ordain priests and priestesses in defiance of the Church is no prophet, while the visionary who submits all claimed supernatural messages to their bishop and accepts the latter's discipline is giving a positive sign. Judging by the reluctance of some of the Old Testament prophets to undertake their mission, many authentic prophets must have stifled the Spirit, that is, refused to speak the words they were given, because they could not face the public ridicule or opposition that is usually offered the prophet.

The special relationship that some individuals have to God is a mystery long recognised by the Jewish people in their high regard for the prophets, and by the Church, which has a formal procedure for recognising such individuals as saints, that is, people whose faithfulness to God allows them to be received into his presence at their death. Many saints are known to have had very unusual experiences of enlightenment, and even of specific and detailed knowledge of God's will and demands. Catholic tradition accepts not only the authenticity and the value of many such 'private revelations', but has always been tolerant of the popular devotions that arise from them in the celebration of saints and in the veneration of the greatest of their number, the Blessed Virgin Mary, who has so often been the messenger of divine Providence. If the main guidance we are given comes to us through the more familiar means of the moral, spiritual and doctrinal teaching of Scripture and the Church, which we have been considering so far, we have yet to open the door on how this mystical tradition impacts specifically on our own times and the future.

Why modern prophets?

Whenever you hear a word from me, warn them in my name.
(Ezk 3:17)

We now live in a time of immense confusion. There are so many different kinds of prophets: secular ones who tell us how to make the most of life in the here-and-now, religious ones who claim secret knowledge that can give adherents the edge over other people in understanding life and becoming part of an elite that is promised salvation in some earthly or spiritual form, and those who merely repeat the Revelation given once and for all by God, which is intended for everyone, which is simple, patently sincere, and which promises more than all the rest added together, namely eternal life with God. This is the message that has to be heard, and which will be heard by those who are ready, even if they have no preconception as to what it is they might be about to hear, and even if they are not seeking in the direction that could lead them naturally to this message. God does not depend upon human channels, but he may sometimes use them. Each turning of an individual towards God is a miracle in itself, and can be accomplished by ways that defy human comprehension. This work of grace is essential for conversion, and yet it is not arbitrary. It comes from God's loving kindness and depends upon the humility and sincerity of the person concerned.

True prophets, however, have never found it easy to get a hearing. Jesus said that a prophet was not honoured in his own country, but today prophets are dismissed with scorn nearly everywhere. In Old Testament times they stoned the prophets, and told them not to prophesy. Today, prophets are turned into figures of fun, even by those who make money from writing books and articles and from making television programmes about them. But even this was prophesied. Isaiah tells us that people will 'have ears and will not hear, eyes and will not see', and the Gospels warned us that there would be false prophets who would have more success in making themselves heard than the true ones, and this because, as St Paul explains, people have ears that itch for novelties. The striking thing about authentic prophecy, and perhaps one of the main reasons why it is so little attended to, is that it tells us nothing new; it repeats what we have been able to read in Scripture, and what we have preserved, if perhaps in a garbled form, in our collective cultural memory. What modern prophecy does is merely to clarify the fittingness of the message and its application to particular times and circumstances.

In exploring the theme of contemporary prophecy in Catholic consciousness, it is impossible to avoid speaking continually of the Blessed Virgin Mary. It is, therefore, striking that Evangelical writers almost never mention her. It is to be hoped that this particular blindness will be removed as the facts of current private revelations to the world become better known. It is even more strange to find prominent Catholic authors apparently deliberately avoiding speaking of Mary's role. McKenzie considers, for example, that there are no grounds for taking the 'Woman adorned with the sun' of the Book of Revelation to represent Mary (McKenzie, 1968, p.41), even though the proclamation of the dogma of the Assumption is closely linked to this text of Scripture. Yocum, who writes only of what he calls 'charismatic prophecy', fails to mention Mary, Fatima or even the phenomenon of contemporary apparitions in a whole work on prophecy (Yocum, 1993). Clearly there is a wider blindness that cannot be ignored. This is an aspect of the Church's beliefs and teachings that needs a separate assessment, and therefore the following chapter will seek to explain why Mary not only continues to occupy such an important place in the Church so long after her earthly life ended, but why she is also such a key figure in gaining any understanding of 'end times' prophecies. It will in fact be shown that she is the main intermediary by whom such prophecies have been proclaimed, first of all to Catholics, but increasingly to Christians of other denominations as well as to non-believers who have been given the grace to receive them.

5

The prophetic role of Mary

Queen of Prophets

Then the sanctuary of God in heaven opened, and the ark of the covenant could be seen inside it ... a great sign appeared in heaven, a woman adorned with the sun, standing on the moon, and with twelve stars on her head for a crown.
(Rv 11:19–12:1)

The Blessed Virgin Mary is linked to messianic prophecies in Scripture, even though she is not named. In Isaiah 7, there is the prophecy of the birth of the Messiah to a virgin. For Christians this is the foretelling of the incarnation, so called because it was the enfleshment of the promised Messiah. The flesh he received was Mary's, the new Ark of the Covenant which contained him. The incarnation is a fact of human history and of Mary's biography as much as it is a theological truth. That is, the incarnation is to be understood in both spiritual and earthly senses. It is a dual reality, and it is Mary who roots the incarnation in earthly life, and thus sets in motion humanity's whole salvation history. This is confirmed for us by the prophecy that Mary herself uttered when she said 'Behold all generation will call me blessed'. Many call her the *Blessed* Virgin Mary today without realising that they are fulfilling a biblical prophecy when they do so.

For Catholics these details are not an optional part of Christian belief. The virginal conception of Jesus is explicitly proclaimed in the Creed. The dogma of the Mother of God is implicit in the Creed, and was defined by the Council of Ephesus in 431 A.D. And the dogmas of the Immaculate Conception of Mary and her bodily Assumption into heaven, though only defined by the Church in the present century, are seen as corollaries of basic Christian beliefs about redemption and resurrection which are also in the Creed, and discernible to the eyes of the believer in Scripture, especially in Revelation 12. These doctrines are crucially important because Mary had a hidden role in the life and mission of Jesus that is being brought progressively to light; this role has become an essential element of the Church's history and mission. She is seen as having intervened in human history in the defeat of the Turks at the Battle of Lepanto in 1571, and in the conversion of Mexico to Christianity following her apparitions to Juan Diego at Guadalupe in 1531, and in a later stage of salvation history at Fatima and at other places of her apparitions to human visionaries. Moreover, the sense of the faithful has constantly attested her divinely-inspired power, wisdom and love, and has demonstrated its fruits by a response of spiritual renewal and holiness of life, especially in the vast numbers of saints and members of religious orders who have modelled their lives upon hers.

Why has the Church given the Blessed Virgin Mary the title 'Queen of Prophets' in its prayers? There is a truth here that needs to be searched out. Instead, we see that Mary is marginalised by many in influential positions in the Church, as well as by most Protestants, while even her enormous cultural significance is discounted by nearly all secular opinion, especially that of many feminists. Yet is it not clear that she is speaking for God, that she has a God-given role in our world, that her apparitions and messages are a call to repentance, to live the Gospel and to turn back to God for the sake of salvation? These are precisely the calls always heard from prophets, but now there is a crescendo in which the quiet, pure voice of Mary rings clear. From all sides there is a sense that a time of decision is coming, and the Blessed Virgin Mary is the one who tells us what needs to be done and, what is more, offers her help in the most essential way. It is Mary who is charged with helping people to respond. Her motive, as in the Gospel, is to bring them to her Son.

This she does by her prayers, by convincing people that they must change, and by inspiring them to holiness. The way she indicates to holiness is by responding to her precepts, her example, and her ministry. Her precepts she gives in her messages, but she is the woman of faith, hope and love that we have always known from the Gospels. There is really no new message. Her example is therefore a perennial one that can be taken up and applied to our lives today. Her ministry is to be the Immaculate One to whom we abandon ourselves, so that we can be changed and sanctified by her prayers and by the power she has been given to mediate graces to souls.

Mary is therefore much more than a prophet. Her prophetic call to follow her is not an impossible ideal, as some argue, but a way of simplicity and truth by which she can lead us more effectively than any other counsellor. It seems that God requires that all recognise the special dignity and role of Mary as the mother of the incarnate God, and therefore the crowned Queen of Heaven and the one who is assured of final victory in her spiritual combat against Satan. The world received Jesus through Mary when he was born in Bethlehem; now it is to receive him through her again when he comes in glory. Her virtues and her actions are fully aligned with the will of God, and she therefore provides a clear way to him. Her acceptability to God is so total that she has the power to win salvation for those who are willing and open to this. As St Louis Marie de Montfort says in his work *True Devotion to Mary*, there are other ways to God, but this is the simplest, and this is the way that God wills everyone to follow (Montfort, 1985). Those who turn to Mary do not abandon Jesus, since she is always with him. Those who obey Mary do not put in question their commitment to Jesus, because her only wish is for him to be loved and worshipped. Only those who recognise the miracle of Mary, her faith, her love, her purity, her holiness, and her spiritual martyrdom, can fully accept her prophetic ministry and confidently follow the way she is leading in our time.

It was in the 1950's that I started to be informed about Marian apparitions and prophecies through the events of Fatima, but this interest later lapsed, together with all my other religious preoccupations, until 1983 when I became aware of Medjugorje, and made a pilgrimage there. Since that time I have been in touch with large numbers of people whose lives have been changed by heeding Mary's prophetic messages, and I have personally met quite a number of the visionaries concerned so that I have had the opportunity to consider my personal response both spiritually and sociologically. I accept the basic truths of these messages, and I believe in the authenticity of Fatima and Medjugorje, as entirely mutually consistent bodies of spiritual teachings that have come to us from God at different times through apparitions of the Virgin Mary. It simply cannot be denied that the Virgin Mary's apparitions in Guadalupe in the sixteenth century, and in this century at Fatima and Medjugorje, have touched millions of lives, have brought about physical healings and spiritual conversions, and have ushered in a new era of faith and practice in whole areas of the world.

My first visit to Medjugorje in January 1984 did not in fact result so much from a strong devotion to the Virgin Mary as from finding it a suitable place for a pilgrimage of thanksgiving for my return to faith in God. It seemed so extraordinary that there should be such a manifestation in a communist country, and yet a moderately accessible one at that time. The pilgrimage's impact, however, was of a totally unexpected degree. After only four days in Medjugorje I had experienced what was effectively a renewal of my spiritual life. Prayer, the Mass, fasting, the role of Mary in the Church, and the importance of spreading the Christian Gospel, all began to open up as new perspectives in my life. When I returned home I wrote articles and gave talks on the messages of Mary in Medjugorje. Then I became editor of a quarterly magazine to promote these, and in the succeeding years I led pilgrimages, became the convenor of the national Network of Medjugorje groups in England, and published a book on the spiritual message of Medjugorje (Plunkett, 1990).

How did all this stem from a few days spent on pilgrimage? My story is by no means unique. I have personally met scores if not hundreds of people who have had comparable experiences through Medjugorje. It is a shrine where spiritual conversions occur constantly, where people turn even from dissolute lives within a few days, often instantaneously, and where practising Christians seem to find a new dimension to their faith and their spiritual lives. Catholics have traditionally drawn a great deal from the example of Mary as the most complete and devoted of the disciples of Jesus, but they are also known for their veneration for the saints, as those who have been exemplary followers of Jesus, and whose prayers are invoked to help those still on the road to salvation. To those who enter this spiritual realm, Mary and the other saints are not mere images or lifeless symbols. They are real persons, serving God in his Kingdom, still open to communication through prayer with believers on earth, and still able to help realise God's plans by their spiritual intervention in response to the prayers of those who turn to them. The veneration given to Mary is different only in degree to that accorded, for example, to St Therese of Lisieux, St Francis of Assisi, or St Thomas More.

The influence of Medjugorje attained worldwide dimensions in less than a decade. The explanation lies in the messages that the Virgin Mary has given through her apparitions. She has always made clear to particular people to whom she appeared the reason why she came. Usually, too, she has come unsolicited, simply choosing a person, or a few people, as her messengers. The messages she has given have essentially reiterated the gospel call to repentance for sin, conversion of life, more ardent prayer, the spreading of God's word to others, and working for the good of neighbours and for peace. At the time of my own first visit to Medjugorje I was curious, but also hopeful. I wanted greater conviction about the reality of God, something more personal than the tradition that had been passed on to me. And I can say that I found it. I cannot really explain what happened, but I developed a faith and a zeal which, however imperfect, have never since then left me or allowed me to think that the Christian life was anything other than an amazing ongoing adventure. I see the messages of Mary through the visionaries of Medjugorje as a prophetic statement to the world. They summon the world back to God. They speak of his goodness, his mercy, his desire that all should know him. They offer a way to God through prayer and detachment from the world, that is the world in the sense of attachments to self-love, self-satisfactions, and materialism. And they give assurance of the presence of Mary as the spiritual mother of all people, whether they are Christian believers of not, in such a way as to be a helper or guide to everyone in their spiritual journey towards God.

Spiritual mother and guide

Do whatever he tells you. (Jn 2:5)

In Medjugorje, Mary is also honoured as the Queen of Peace, because she is teaching believers through her spiritual messages that the way to peace is through prayer and personal change which can then flow out to the world. Peace is the spiritual conquest of self and the total acceptance of God's will. As the spiritual mother of all humanity, Mary is summoning us to return to God. She has been given great power as an intercessor, that is, one who prays and can obtain God's grace and mercy for us. Mary, the sinless mother who was responsible for the human upbringing of Jesus, is thereby able to assist us in becoming more like her Son and in turning to him. She looks for nothing for herself, but acts always in God's interests. If the infinite quality of the love between Jesus and Mary could be more widely understood there would be no more complaints from Christians about Mary distracting us from Jesus. She would never want that. Her path leads to God. This means that her existence has one overriding priority: to worship her Creator. She is a figure of hope, 'a radiant model for those who entrust themselves with all their hearts to the promises of God' (John Paul II, 1994, para 48). In all her messages, and especially at Medjugorje, she stresses this by warning against discouragement or dwelling on prophecies of doom, and saying that those who believe in God and place their trust in him have nothing to fear.

The messages of Medjugorje contain both their own characteristic spirituality and a programme of guidance. They are words of holiness, words from Heaven. Because we live on earth, and because we are compromised in so many ways by worldly attachments, we do not find it easy to recognise the depth of meaning of the messages. Some have even dismissed them as banal or repetitive. This only shows how much we can lack the spirit of holiness which would enable us to see in the words the depth of meaning and the truth which characterise all heavenly language. If the angels can endlessly repeat their hosannas, how is it that we can think of Mary's constant counsels as repetitive? Would it not be more honest to admit that it is we who *repeatedly* fail to understand, to learn, and to change?

As the years pass since the apparitions began, a significant fact begins to emerge. Perhaps not since the Gospels themselves has there been such a complete work of spiritual guidance as in the Medjugorje messages, certainly not one that speaks as directly and powerfully to the people of today's world. Mary herself calls Medjugorje a 'fountain of grace' (13 November 1986). If she is able to guide those willing to follow her to paradise (25 September 1994), there is a vital resource which too many Christians ignore. But Mary is much more than a guide. She is a mother. And it is with this special reality that we must begin if we want to understand Mary, the mother Jesus so generously shared with all humanity when he said from the cross to the two people in the world who most loved him: 'Woman behold your son.... Behold your mother' (Jn 19:26–27). And even before that decisive moment on Calvary, Mary had been guiding people towards holiness and truth, and towards her Son. Had she not told the servants at the marriage feast of Cana: 'Do whatever he tells you ' (Jn 2:5)? And she has continued to say the same to countless people down the ages. The messages of Medjugorje say no more than this in essence: 'Do what he has already told you in the Gospels'.

Many who live committed Christian lives seek counsellors or spiritual guides to help them, as their predecessors have always done in the past, but today this is not always possible. Spiritual guides are lacking or are overwhelmed with demands. Mary meets this need. She offers guidance in doing what Jesus says, but guidance adapted to a world in which people have turned away from disciplined lives, and from spiritual pursuits and prayer. She suggests a rule of life, and calls this living her messages, the spiritual advice that she has been giving in Medjugorje since June 1981 to lead people to holiness and peace. Other guides in today's world promise tangible benefits, secret knowledge, security from disasters, personal fulfilment, wealth, health, even power, but of course most are false prophets, preaching only one or other form of idolatry, and the end is frequently disaster. Mary is not a guru. Her guidance has a quite different quality. And there is only one word for it: motherly. Mary offers love, tears, pleading, hopes and her constant devotion to Jesus:

> *Dear children, today again I am calling you to prayer. I need your prayers so that God may be glorified through all of you. Dear children, I beg you to obey me and live according to your mother's call, because I call you only out of love for you so that I may help you. Thank you for having responded to my call. (16 January 1986)*

It is so natural that a mother should guide that is is astonishing how few realise it is actually happening. And this is because, like everything else in the order of grace, all is gratuitous, nothing is imposed. People are not asked to be uniform, to lose their identities, to follow blindly. Everything is explained, and all are free to choose. Yet when she calls people to put God first in their lives (25 November 1992), Mary is asking them to do exactly what she has done herself. She knows from experience that this is the way to salvation, that it is Jesus's way. And she knows that when all take the same way God's plan of salvation will be fulfilled.

How is this guidance to be applied? In order to provide a simple and concrete spiritual rule of life for all to follow, Mary proposes the example of Medjugorje as the parish to be observed and emulated. We do not become saints by doing things, even very good things. We grow in holiness only if the things we do express genuine faith and love. Therefore, even more important than a spiritual rule is the consciousness of God that must underlie it. This is carefully explained in message after message. We are to learn from imitating Jesus and Mary, by keeping peace in our own hearts and offering witness to the world to consolidate the victory won by Jesus on the cross. All this is the spiritual journey that tests us and gives us the opportunity to become holy, to become united to

Summary of the Blessed Virgin's teaching in Medjugorje

The most insistent messages are concerned with conversion, faith and reconciliation with God. The principal points of emphasis are:

- decide for God (25 January 1990)
- through prayer of the heart (30 May 1985)
- through surrendering to God (25 February 1990)
- through changing our lives totally, by daily conversion (25 February 1993)
- the world is being fought for by Satan (25 September 1986)
- resist Satan through prayer, fasting and complete surrender to God (4 September 1986)
- by praying for the gifts of the Holy Spirit (17 May 1986)
- by living each day the messages Mary gives us (22 November 1984)
- so as to receive the graces promised: understanding (25 January 1987)
- joy (25 February 1987)
- holiness (25 May 1987)
- love (25 June 1988)
- and peace (25 June 1987)

God, not out of our own strength, but through humility, and abandonment to God.

Pilgrimage is just the outward form of an interior journey on which all are embarked, a journey in the spirit to meet God in our lives, our thoughts, our families, our jobs, our community, or in our health, or wealth and all the other circumstances of life. Lifestyle is also a journey. If charity has grown cold, there is the chance to reverse this by love and service to each other. If apostasy abounds, there is the opportunity to pray for unbelievers and to witness to them. One of the visionaries of Medjugorje, Mirjana, has been asked by the Virgin Mary to pray especially for unbelievers.

Once, when Mirjana was asked who were the unbelievers, she replied: 'Anyone who does not see heaven as their home and God as their Father'. Each one who is a believer in these terms is given occasions to evangelise, to speak of God, and to help build God's Kingdom.

> Everything you do and everything you possess give over to God so that he can take control in your life as King of all that you possess. That way, through me, God can lead you into the depths of the spiritual life. My dear children, do not be afraid because I am with you even when you think Satan is in control and that there is no way out. I am bringing peace to you.
> (25 July 1988)

Mary encourages everyone in all these endeavours as she encouraged the first Christians. Indeed the people of Medjugorje and Bosnia had been through the early Christian experiences of Pentecost, persecution and the Diaspora, in the 1980's, and since then have seen the spreading of the message to the wider world, leading to a movement of renewal in the Church. The complete preservation of Medjugorje from the effects of the war that followed in Bosnia is an important sign. This horrifyingly brutal war warns us that reconciliation and peace are needed everywhere. There is no reason why other societies should consider themselves immune from such violence. However, one keynote of the Medjugorje messages is their hopefulness. Mary once said to the locutionary Jelena, when she was reading a book about the secrets of the apparitions in Fatima:

> Don't think about wars, chastisements, evil. It is when you concentrate on these things that you are on the way to enter into them. Your responsibility is to accept divine peace, to live it. (n.d.)

Medjugorje consistently reflects this positive attitude, because the messages do not sow seeds of alarm and despondency, but encourage hope and reliance on God rather than on human solutions. The whole Medjugorje message is one of hope for salvation, of trust in God. This is why it is unreasonable for it to be dismissed as unnecessary or lacking in spiritual acuity or depth. The world is terribly in need of hope, yet does not know where to turn. Medjugorje acts as a school for holiness for pilgrims. Those who have travelled there in a spirit of faith have learnt about prayer, the word of God, the Mass, the rosary. They have sensed very specially the love of God and the spiritual motherhood of Mary, and have felt the call to grow. Those who respond to this call become holier, closer to God, and everything else in their lives then begins to change. They will be better apostles and witnesses, more loyal to the Church, and more committed to living Christian lives. It is a question of deepening their understanding of what the Virgin Mary offers, so that they are transformed. Rather than becoming experts on Medjugorje to be able to pass on new ideas and information to others, they must become deeper persons reaching out in a spirit of faith and love.

This is the ideal that Mary sets before us by restating the gospel values and truths taught and lived by Jesus. She is not inventing something new. She is confirming what we already know in our hearts and consciences, but have neglected. This is the way for everyone to live. Quite clearly, too, this is the way she lived, in the spirit of the submission of her will to God, when asked by the Archangel Gabriel to become the mother of the Redeemer, the one who would support Jesus throughout his life and public ministry. This is the demeanour of one who in the early Church was the ever-present human bond of unity and peace, whose prayerfulness in the Upper Room had consolidated and consecrated the Church at its foundation. Is this going too far? No, because Mary had borne the body of Jesus, presenting him at the temple, and now she consecrates the Church, his mystical body, by her presence among the apostles, and in our time by her coming and her prophetic messages.

Listening to her words, we can reflect firstly that it is extraordinary that we should actually be hearing words from Heaven. If we really believe this then each syllable must be of the utmost importance, and none without significance. So the first point would be to listen as attentively as possible, and to try to understand, in prayer, the meaning of each message and the import of all the messages bearing ultimately upon the theme of peace in its fullness. Secondly, we could consider the Medjugorje messages as the Gospel applied to our times, and pointing us back to the Gospel that we have been ignoring. Recognising the parallels between the messages and Scripture is essential and extremely valuable for learning to live them.[21] There may be many ways of interpreting the messages and identifying the priorities that they suggest, according to our individual personalities and circumstances. It is one thing to listen, another to understand, and yet a third actually to live the messages. The depth at which the messages are assimilated depends on openness, good will, and conversion of heart, so that we are genuinely changed. It is not a question of an external conformity to the messages, but of a transformation that affects our minds and our hearts, and thus impacts on our faith, our behaviour and the spiritual quality of our whole existence.

There are many movements that contribute to the work of the Church, but the worldwide renewal of hearts and of the Church itself would be much more problematic without the guidance and intercession of Mary in this special way. Some will reject such a view, but that is a part of the problem. What have they to put in the place of this marvellous plan of God? There are, for example, those who respond to the lifestyle counsels of the Blessed Virgin Mary concerning prayer, fasting, confession, Mass, rosary, and the Scriptures by claiming that we need instead to become more conscious of social, political, geopolitical and ideological movements, and even to become involved in these secular struggles. Is this just another form of the liberal thought that wants to confine spirituality to a horizontal plane, or is this something new that offers a combination of vertical and horizontal spirituality? Christians undoubtedly have a global responsibility, and should pray for both the particular and the universal. They may indeed need to become more critical observers of the social and political scene in order to know what to pray for, or rather to better focus their prayers on God's specific wishes for our world.

However, many Catholics have come to accept the prophetic messages of Mary at Fatima and at Medjugorje as announcing a critical time for the world, but at a wholly different level from social and political affairs. It is a time when everyone will have to say where they stand, and only those who have begun to search in their consciences will be able to respond. It seems that it is particularly to those souls that are already prepared that any prophetic signs will bring the last stage of conviction. The progress of evil in the world is so cataclysmic, and so contrary to God's will for his creation, that it cannot conceivably continue. Some change, some intervention in the whole situation, seems inevitable, and indeed has been prophesied, even though we do not know when or how it will occur. As far as the Blessed Virgin Mary is concerned, it seems undeniable that the influence of her messages has already led huge numbers of people to reverse their way of life, to increase their spiritual commitment, and to pray with greatly increased faith and zeal. These renewed Christians are now placing God and his Kingdom first. This is not a sect engaged in Mariolatry, since Mary is the mother who leads all to Jesus. It is much more like the life of the early Church, which is a model of Christianity that all believers are agreed is the one they are called to follow.

6

The end times

The Day of the Lord

> *Watch yourselves, or your hearts will be coarsened with debauchery and drunkenness and the cares of life, and that day will be sprung on you suddenly, like a trap.* (Lk 21:34)

There are close to a hundred Bible texts referring to a future day of reckoning, often called 'the Day of the Lord' or the 'Day of Judgement', or simply 'that day'. The context usually appears to suggest a time when everything will finally be revealed, judged, or decided, as for example in 'Cry aloud, for the Day of the Lord is coming; his the dominion, his the doom' (Is 13:6). Many of these texts are specific instances of how God's justice is meted out, or events which seem to be warnings for the future. Thus, Ezechiel tells of the Lord's punishment of the people for their idolatry: there will be the four-fold curse of sword, famine, wild beasts and pestilence, and only a remnant will survive (Ezk 14:21–22). The destruction of Babylon is the metaphor for the final retribution to be awarded by the divine judge, in Isaiah 13, and in the Book of Revelation 16–18. If we are wondering whether such biblical passages might be no more than a stylistic convention or simply expressions of common fears and longings, we have to enter the difficult terrain of discernment. That is, our response to the proverbial sandwich board announcement: 'Repent, for the end of the world is nigh', can be either the relaxed jocularity of the sophisticated atheist, the smiling shrug of the tolerant agnostic, or the thoughtfully pursed lips of the believer.

Even from the conventional Christian standpoint the interpretation of biblical prophecy is very often controversial. Does the 'Day of the Lord' mean the end of the world, or could it be the messianic age, the time before the end that seems to be foreseen in prophecy when the world will know an era of peace? If the latter, then end times prophecies could refer to a time of purification, a time of renewal and hope, not of disaster or of finality. Both interpretations need to be borne in mind, because both have similar spiritual implications: they demand our change of heart. Many scholars, like McKenzie, the author of the reputed *Dictionary of the Bible* (McKenzie, 1968, p.40), confidently exclude consideration of a link between the Book of Revelation and the contemporary era, and yet this is the very contention of large numbers of modern prophets and writers who seek to argue its relevance to current conditions and problems. In many prophetic messages the coming of the Lord in glory, his presence already among us, all are common threads. Although there appear to be no scriptural clues as to dates when the day will come, there are several warnings to be constantly ready, since it will come suddenly, 'like a trap'. An apostasy by large numbers of former believers, leaving only a small faithful remnant, or the fidelity of the *anawin,* the humble people of God, are also common reference points.

Moreover, judgement is an essential element of God's plan, both in the immediate and as a long-term prospect, when everyone must show their worth or merit, according to what God expects of his creatures. This teleological element should not surprise us, because we learn through revelation in the Scriptures that there is to be a final judgement, a time when all will be brought to completion. In this sense there is a definite chronology, known only to the Father, according to which all genuine prophecy will eventually find confirmation. Individually, we may be preoccupied by our own lives which are subject to more immediate constraints and timescales, but collectively we are awaiting this final outcome. Either way, we must discern God's word to us, and the response it demands of us.

The Jews, like Christians, recognise a hastening of the times. For many of them, the coming of the Messiah is fast approaching, either in the form of a person, in the Orthodox interpretation, or as an era of justice and peace, as the Reformed tradition sees it. Christians are expecting the second coming of Jesus the Messiah, as a time of decision without precedent. The prophet traces this consciousness, feeds and guides it, and recalls how this is the fulfilment of promises made long ago. A certain convergence of Jewish and Christian expectations, even a fusion of divine purposes becomes conceivable, though God is not limited to what can be humanly imagined. None the less it is remarkable that there is a similar expectancy in many quarters and in different faiths. New Testament writing reflects the belief that the Old Covenant has been fulfilled by the New, and not revoked. The Jews are seen as having suffered a blindness with respect to the recognising of Jesus as the Messiah, but one that is only temporary. This blindness is spoken of by the Jewish Scriptures: 'For on you has Yahweh poured a spirit of lethargy; he has closed your eyes (the prophets), he has veiled your heads (the seers)' (Is 29:10). St Paul cites this verse, and adds: 'and they are still like that today' (Rm 11:8). But he goes on to say: 'One section of Israel has become blind, but this will only last until the pagan world has entered, and then after this the rest of Israel will be saved as well' (Rm 11:25–26). This 'illumination' of the Jews is therefore still for the future for most, but it is taken as certain by Paul that the Jews will turn to Christ, and acknowledge the accomplishment of God's promise in him.

Already we see the phenomenon of the Messianic Jews, Jews who are coming in substantial numbers to accept Jesus as their hoped-for Messiah. For the great majority of believing Jews this moment has not arrived, but the 'ingathering', the Aliyah, of the Jews, through the formation of the State of Israel, is seen by many as a sign of the end times. In their interpretation of Scripture, Orthodox Jews recognise the prophecy of Moses as the final destiny of their people:

> ...Yahweh your God will bring back your captives, he will have pity on you and gather you once again out of all the peoples where Yahweh your God has scattered you. (Dt 30:3)

This prophecy of the return from exile has been honoured by the Law of Return of the State of Israel, guaranteeing all Jews the right to settle in Israel. While Jews converted to Christianity are found in many denominations, and they have certainly made an enormous contribution to the Catholic Church, as in the case of the ministry of Cardinal Lustiger, the present Archbishop of Paris, there are many who prefer to stand outside the denominations, awaiting Christian reunion. Some of these consider that they thus form a 'Hebrew' church. It seems fitting that the reconciliation of the Jews and the Christians should be preceded by the unity of the Christians, and it is no doubt significant that Pope John Paul places such store by developments towards Christian unity by the end of the Millennium (John Paul II, 1994, p.151). Modern Church sources have resisted speaking of the 'conversion' of the Jews, and the Council Fathers at Vatican II preferred to say that 'the Church awaits that day, known to God alone, on which all peoples will address the Lord with a single voice ...' *Nostra Aetate*, para 4).

Much of the Bible is apocalyptic, up to twenty per cent according to some estimates. Although I have not attempted such calculations myself, I am quite ready to credit them. If one examines Isaiah, for example, and notices the way in which the then contemporary events take on an apocalyptic character, nearly the whole book can be seen as a preparation for the life, death and resurrection of Christ, and all that would flow from this. The Babylon of Isaiah 13 and 14 is the historical Chaldean city, but it is also the symbolic gathering place of God's enemies, who must be spiritually destroyed, 'root and branch'. Isaiah 47 elaborates details of God's anger with Babylon, daughter of the Chaldeans, who is to be punished and reduced from her glory as sovereign lady of the nations. This punishment is because Babylon had mistreated God's people, and the form that it will take will bring widowhood and deprivation of her children to Babylon in a single day, despite all the seemingly magic power of her spells. Babylon was misled by her confidence in her knowledge and wisdom, her conviction that no one could better her or find her out. 'Unforeseen ruin will suddenly descend on you' (Is 47:11), and none of her advisers or prophets will be able to help her.

These passages no doubt reflect a specific historical context, but their prophetic value can surely not be ignored. The virgin daughter of Babylon is to be dethroned and humiliated. The one who expected to inherit will never do so. The powers rising up to administer the earth will be defeated. What has been concealed is going to be revealed and will be the cause of great shame. The secrets of human power are shameful, ungodly. God is angry with the misuse to which she has put her life, her power, her opportunities, her blessings, and her freedom. She must now surrender her interests, with no one to help her withstand the fate in store. The Holy One of Israel rejects her. She is judged fairly for what she has done, and for what she has failed to do. She thoughtlessly exploited and mistreated without any mercy. She trusted in witchcraft, that is, knowledge which is not at God's service. Too much has happened which God can only reject. He can no longer sift good from bad; all is rotten, putrefying. Her husband, the source of her wealth, power, strength, and position, is dismissed. Her children, the fruit of that union, of its intelligence, beauty, creativity, and desire, are cast aside. The wages of utter selfishness are to be disappointed, and all efforts to save herself are unavailing.

It cannot be surprising that a set of books compiled to record God's relationship to his chosen people should dwell so much on the final outcomes of the conflict between good and evil, truth and falsehood, hope and despair: that is, salvation or damnation. Religious believers know that life on earth is about something, but few human beings can escape speculating about this issue. We are, in practice, obliged to decide whether our lives are solely concerned with the people and things we currently encounter, or whether they are also, or even principally, about a future trial and judgement and other unknowns which we can only perceive 'as in a glass darkly'. Applied to our own times these texts seem to spell the doom of our Western world. So much false knowledge, so much seeming magic, so much confidence in science and technology, in politics and government, and yet it is unavailing; it will not prevent disaster. Obviously, the point of these passages from Isaiah in a contemporary interpretation could be to sound the alarm, so that believers begin to do what they have failed so far to do, that is to observe, listen, pray, and prepare spiritually, which means also to dispose their human affairs differently.

Are we living in the end times?

> *Take the fig tree as a parable: as soon as its twigs grow supple and its leaves come out, you know that summer is near. So with you when you see all these things: know that he is near, at the very gates.* (Mt 24:32–33)

There is undoubtedly a preoccupation in today's world with decoding mysteries and secrets that might reveal where the world is going to end up. To exemplify this, with former Soviet republics resisting Russian efforts to reestablish their power, we can be forgiven for getting a queasy sensation that the whole ex-USSR is edging closer to self-destruction, or towards the edge of a precipice from which they will tumble down on the rest of us. And indeed prophets of doom are plentiful nowadays. The perilous state of the world constantly features in the ecology literature, in New Age prophecies, or in the warnings from many claimed visions being reported around the world, as well as in much more conventional Church sources. Few people, after all, have a more consistently, if measured, apocalyptic tone to their observations than Pope John Paul II. In 1976, before he became Pope, he said at a Eucharistic Conference in Philadelphia:

> We are now standing at the brink of the final confrontation between the Gospel and the anti-Gospel, the Church and the antichrist, and this is a trial which the whole community of faith must take up.

What is a reasonable person to do in response? Can supposedly prophetic messages and people's reactions to them be accounted for psychologically? Can some be ascribed to a peasant-like ignorance of the seers that is referred to sneeringly by some commentators? Are many of them simply due to misunderstanding or overly speculative interpretations of the Bible?

If we have any inkling or belief that there is such a world

of unknowns, whether it encompasses knowledge, experiences or a whole different dimension of existence, we are likely to feel unsettled whenever we encounter those who 'know', or who claim to have privileged access to sources of knowledge, or who try to recruit us to their world outlook or view of the future. We need to be acutely discerning about the view we take, but this does not entail being totally sceptical, as if to claim that we can never be persuaded by speculative ideas or mystical views of life and spiritual matters stemming from private revelation. The question has therefore to be posed: is it reasonable in human terms to reject the apocalyptic from consideration, to ignore thoughts of end times or of 'last things'? Contemporary prophecy, as I understand it, is largely an underlining of scriptural prophecy or, to put it the other way round, scriptural prophecies are illuminated by those in our own day. The prophetic messages of Scripture needed to have their link to our time brought out in this way, because until a few decades ago they would not have been read as having contemporary relevance. No one in the pre-Vatican II Church could have imagined the apostasy and the dissolution of the Church that has occurred within a single generation. In this sense contemporary prophecy proves its authenticity by its faithfulness to Scripture. It is a retelling of Scripture, not some other story.

A striking feature of many religions' conclusions about the world in our day is in fact their agreement that we are moving towards 'end times', not necessarily the 'end of the world' but a time of decision that is wholly spiritual in nature, when we will judge ourselves, before we come to face divine judgement. In the Christian tradition, such apocalyptic conclusions are formed not only from Scripture, but also through the astonishing variety of contemporary prophecies by seers claiming to have received visions, apparitions and messages from God or from the Blessed Virgin Mary. The messages of Fatima have undoubtedly been the most noteworthy of these prophecies, together with those more recently from Medjugorje. The justification for taking these particular contemporary prophecies seriously is partly the number and unimpeachability of the young, healthy and innocent witnesses, but even more because the signs of our own times are like the branches of the fig tree in being so strongly aligned with the biblical prophecies, that they echo and explain them within a contemporary frame of reference.

More specifically, many of them refer to conflicts arising in the Church. Why is there division or dissent in the Church? It must be because the Church is in the forefront of the spiritual battle to decide the future of humanity, whether it is to be won or lost for Christ. Without the Church there is no salvation. Salvation comes through Jesus Christ; and his teaching, his good news, is being carried forward by the Church. The Church is the ark protecting souls from Satan, who attacks the priesthood, the Eucharist, the family, and everything that is sacred. The power of Satan shows in rebellion within the Church, in apostasy, in conspiracy, whether among secular powers that seek to marginalise the Church or in ecclesiastical circles, in the New Age movement that offers false gods for human worship, in forms of feminism that go beyond issues of peace and justice towards self-idolatry, and in compromise by Christian theologians over morals and doctrine that justify new teachings as if Christianity were not the definitive revelation of God through Jesus Christ.

There is much scepticism about what is currently seen as millennialism in the religious world associated with the end of the twentieth century.[22] While it is well known that at the approach of the year 1000 A.D. there was a rush of 'end of the world' movements, it has to be recognised that it is a feature of the teachings of Christianity, and indeed of other faiths, that human life on earth will not go on for ever, and certainly not as long as could be scientifically imagined. Christianity expects an intervention by God and a time of judgement, and the early Christian writers thought that this time was coming soon in human terms. Now many reject the possibility that there will ever be such a time. This view is actually unreasonable, since we all know that we must individually die, and that this will complete whatever life's work we will have achieved. We cannot take much solace from the fact that human life goes on beyond our personal lives unless we believe that there is some way in which our eternal fortunes are taken up in another life. This is the Christian belief that lies behind apocalyptic speculation, such as millennialism, but it can hardly be dismissed as alarmist or unreasonable precisely because for every human being death is always looming, however much unnoticed or denied.

I do not believe that I personally was led back to Christian faith by an awareness of mortality, but I do now acknowledge it as a factor in my faith. Not only do I see life as a time of continual moral decision-making, a time of spiritual struggle as I choose in conscience between right or wrong, but I believe that this life viewed spiritually is principally a preparation for death, judgement and the hereafter, and I take seriously the apocalyptic warnings of a time of personal and collective judgement that are repeatedly recorded in Scripture. Creation is a work of God with a purpose, and at the heart of that purpose is the moral and spiritual life of human beings, who were created with the particular destiny of being free to choose to know, love and serve their Creator. The work of God thus has a finite aspect, one that is implied in the mortality of each human being, but also more definitively in the 'ending' of our world, however obscure we may find that notion.

The Old Testament prophets recognised the coming times when true belief would be all but eliminated, and the New Testament speaks of apocalyptic signs of the times that would come when faith would almost disappear, when beliefs would be confused, and when other events would so trouble people that they would be duped by false prophets, and be afraid and desperate before world disasters and conflicts. Such prophecies feature in the Gospels, and especially in Matthew 24 where, in what is either a very elaborate set of poetic metaphors or a timeless language explaining cosmic matters which are intended as a clear warning, Jesus graphically details the signs of the end times.

It is in fact Matthew 24 to which the Virgin Mary referred in a message given to Fr Stefano Gobbi, an Italian priest who for a quarter of a century has claimed to be receiving prophetic inner messages, or locutions, that are followed by thousands of priests and bishops in the Marian Movement of Priests.[23] In a message to Fr Gobbi, on the last day of 1992, Mary referred to herself as the 'Prophetess of these last times', and set out to explain the relevance of the chapter

Matthew 24: Signs of the end times

When the disciples ask Jesus: 'What will be the sign of your coming and of the end of the world?' his reply can be summarised as follows:

- there will be false prophets claiming to be Christs
- there will be wars, famines and earthquakes
- there will be persecution of the Church, and some will fall away
- there will be lawlessness and 'love in most men will grow cold'
- the Gospel will be proclaimed to the whole world
- there will be a usurping by the 'disastrous abomination'
- the sun will be darkened and stars will fall from the sky
- the sign of the Son of Man will appear in heaven
- the Son of Man will come accompanied by angels and the trumpet will sound

from Matthew's Gospel and of certain texts in St Peter's and St Paul's writings, which she revealed were being 'fulfilled in these years' through the spread of apostasy, wars, persecution, sacrilege, including the temporary suppression of the Mass, and miraculous events in the heavens. She also speaks of the coming full manifestation of the antichrist (Marian Movement of Priests, 1995).

All the signs are that a time will come, and may already have begun, when the Church will nearly be destroyed both from outside and from within. The struggle involving the Church is a spiritual one between the forces of good and evil, and we choose which side we are on with virtually every breath we breathe. If Christians do not believe in the prophecies offered them by Scripture, is it likely that they will believe modern prophets, or that they will avoid being deceived by false prophets? There are many indications that we could be living in the times of false gospels, false prophets and false christs, of which the Scriptures explicitly warn, and it is worth noting that all four evangelists, and St Peter in his second letter, warn against false prophets. There

An 'end times' scenario?

- false prophets are everywhere, like sheep disguised as 'ravening wolves' (Mt 7:15)
- 'the way of truth will be brought into disrepute on their account' (2 P 2:2)
- they will even 'deceive the elect' (Mk 13:22).
- the time has come when people are not content with 'sound teaching', when 'instead of listening to the truth, they will turn to myths' (2 Tm 4: 3–4)
- Christians are confronted by 'unbelievers whose minds the god of this world has blinded' (2 Co 4:4), and by orthodox doctrines being eroded, as dissident theologians and other leaders publicly question or explain away mysteries, miracles and practices of devotion that attest a transcendent God
- many Christians take up elements of 'doctrines that come from the devils' (1 Tm 4:1) seeking to improve upon Christianity with new teachings about God as the divine power within us, and other pantheistic theories
- 'a deceptive show of signs and portents' (2 Th 2:9) is evident in the drug and rock music cultures, for example using hallucinations and cursing with subliminal satanic incantations, in the practice of witchcraft, in the psychological kidnapping practised by certain cults, and in the astrological obsessions of the New Age movement
- the world is full of gurus and credos that sweep people into beliefs and lifestyles that contradict Christianity, in spite of the scriptural warning not to be cheated with 'empty rational philosophy based on the principles of this world' (Col 2:8).

are numerous passages in the New Testament that describe graphically the state of confusion, apostasy, and religious indifferentism that will ensue and overtake the Church. And could any conceivable scenario for the 'end times' be more scripturally warranted than what can be observed today?

It is apparent that there is no consensus about the existence of a transcendent, personal God, let alone the nature of the spiritual dimension to human life. Rationalists deny them, and many Christian believers seem to be in retreat in affirming such truths unequivocally. How then does an orthodox religious outlook contend with such spiritual confusion and the sustained opposition of secularism? Is it possible to continue to assert traditional beliefs and values? Out of a fear of being seen as over-reacting or intolerant, very many believers do not dare to proclaim their faith or even to protest at its marginalisation. Christians long for a more courageous lead from their shepherds, always excepting Pope John Paul II and those many pastors, and even martyrs, who have endured persecution out of loyalty to their faith. But what single Christian can claim not to have a similar duty? Scripture points out that there will be a great revolt (2 Th 2:3), people will abandon 'divine truth for a lie' (Rm 1:25), and that 'the man who stands firm to the end will be saved' (Mt 24:13). It does not say that those who stand by, or give way, who compromise, or who embrace new teachings, will be saved. The *Catechism of the Catholic Church* endorses the literal value of these scriptural prophecies:

> Before Christ's second coming the Church must pass through a final trial that will shake the faith of many believers. The persecution that accompanies her pilgrimage on earth will unveil the 'mystery of iniquity' in the form of a religious deception offering men an apparent solution to their problems at the price of apostasy from the truth. (CCC, 675)

The problem of discernment

> *Never try to suppress the Spirit, or treat prophecy with contempt; think before you do anything - hold on to what is good and avoid every form of evil.* (1 Th 5:19–22)

Although I am writing about almost entirely Catholic sources, there are Protestant authors who write within the Evangelical tradition, which is more strictly scriptural in its points of reference, who reach many of the same conclusions about the times we are living in, namely that we are approaching the end times, when the world is being called to repentance under the impending threat of God's justice.[24] I gladly acknowledge this work, and particularly the contribution made by Clifford Hill, though I believe that it reveals many problems of spiritual discernment. We can make the Bible say more or less whatever we want, and the guide given to Catholic Christians by the discernment of the Church, while often slow to take effect, is a vital guarantee. The Holy Spirit cannot be divided, and although human sinfulness often makes us ambiguous and erroneous, the faith that the Spirit guides us to the truth is a consoling one that ensures that we cannot remain lost in error if we pay heed to the Church. Hill appeals to the Church to wake up and assume a prophetic lead, but he ties the Church's hands behind its back by placing his trust in human agents rather than in what the Spirit is saying to the churches (Rv 2 and 3). There are no doubt many inspired prophets in this tradition, but how one decides whom to trust is a major problem that is not even addressed by Hill, except in terms of a faithfulness to Scripture that is not verifiable in the Evangelical tradition.

It follows that some standard of discernment is needed to know which prophets or prophecies can be confidently regarded as authentic. Hitherto, the Catholic position has been clear. Canon Law has been understood as permitting the investigation of any mystical occurrence, such as a vision, allocution or apparition, provided that it carries no implications that undermine or contradict the faith and moral teachings of the Catholic Church, which Catholics regard as infallible. Naturally, indications of authenticity in the personality, circumstances and claims of any visionary must be scrutinised. Here the requirement is not so much impressive arguments as consistency with Church teaching, even if at times less stressed areas of teaching. Thus, visionaries who strongly endorse Marian devotion, devotion to the Sacred Heart of Jesus, who are loyal to the Pope and to the Church, who call for prayer, particularly the rosary, who speak of the importance of the Mass and of the Holy Eucharist, or who teach the importance of surrender to God and obeying his will, are unlikely to engage in false teachings on other points. Of course this is not an infallible test. The scriptural counsel is that we should not try to suppress prophecy, but judge it by its fruits. That is, we find the truth of prophecy by its impact on the life of the local Church and beyond, on people's spiritual lives, and the incidence of physical healings or other such manifestations of an intrinsically good nature.

Even in secular reports of alleged mystical phenomena, note is often taken of the official position taken by the Catholic Church. The Church is known to treat such matters with extreme caution, and never to make speedy decisions of approval. The practice in the first place is to leave the discernment of the authenticity of supernatural events to the local bishop. It was thus that some of the earlier modern apparitions, including La Salette and Fatima, received ecclesiastical approval despite initial set-backs and delays. In recent years local bishops have given credit to particular visionaries, such as Sr Agnes in Akita, Japan, Maria Esperanza Medrano de Bianchini in Venezuela, and the visionaries of Kibeho in Rwanda. The messages to Fr Gobbi appear with various local imprimaturs, and are obviously regarded with favour by large numbers of bishops. These are probably therefore among the 'safest' of all the modern prophetic messages, and can provide a benchmark for many of the others. There are also claimed private revelations which are currently tolerated by the Church without any definitive ruling as to their authenticity having yet been given. These include those claimed by the visionaries of Medjugorje, Renato Baron in Schio, Italy, Christina Gallagher in Ireland, Patrick Rushe and Patrick O'Kane (the two Patricks) in Northern Ireland, Julia Kim in Naju, Korea, and Patricia Menezes in London. In the cases of Christina and Patricia, both are currently the subject of ecclesiastical study, but meanwhile the houses of prayer they have founded are being permitted to function.

Some other apparitions are officially contested by the Church. These include Garabandal, Spain, to which successive bishops have been opposed, including most recently the Bishop of Santander, in a statement dated 11 October 1996 in which he says that he accepts the (negative) decision of his predecessors, and also the messages of Vassula Ryden, where the Congregation for the Doctrine of the Faith (CDF)[25] has twice reiterated its denial of their supernatural character, most recently in a strongly worded Press release, which quotes Cardinal Ratzinger as stating that:

> ... the faithful are not to regard the messages of Vassula Ryden as divine revelations, but only as her personal meditations', that these meditations include 'elements that are negative in the light of Christian doctrine', and that therefore 'Pastors and the faithful are asked to exercise serious spiritual discernment in this matter and to preserve the purity of the faith, morals and spiritual life, not by relying on alleged revelations but by following the revealed Word of God and the directives of the Church's Magisterium.
>
> (*Osservatore Romano*, 4 December 1996)

This passage is quoted at length because it raises wider issues about the attention that should be paid to any 'alleged revelations'. Although 'approved' revelations do not incur stricture, the statement is incomplete because, by referring only to 'following the revealed Word of God and Church directives', it leaves in limbo major prophetic messages, like those of Fr Gobbi and even Fatima, as regards what response is advised for Catholics.

In a second part of its Press release on the 'Ryden Notification', the CDF widens its attention still further and appears to restrict the circulation of writings and messages resulting from 'alleged private revelations' beyond what has been assumed by many since Canon Law on this point was relaxed by Pope Paul VI in 1966. Such possible strictures, that would seem to require all relevant writings to be submitted to the judgement of bishops, do appear to question what has become normal practice in the Church in recent years, and will undoubtedly need further clarification than that available at the time of writing. In the meantime, Catholics who desire to follow Church guidance are at something of a loss in those cases where a private revelation has not yet been conclusively examined officially, but has attracted wide attention and popular approval, and is showing positive fruits. This is, for example, the situation of Medjugorje, which provides a vital test case for the procedures proposed by the CDF Press release.

The case of Medjugorje

> *A sound tree cannot bear bad fruit, nor a rotten tree bear good fruit. Any tree that does not produce good fruit is cut*

down and thrown on the fire. I repeat, you will be able to tell them by their fruits. (*Mt 7:18–20*)

The local bishop of Mostar, like his predecessor, remains adamantly disapproving of the Medjugorje apparitions, while cardinals, bishops and even allegedly the Pope himself, express firm support, hundreds of them having made pilgrimages to the site.[26] When the matter was referred to the Yugoslav bishops they found 'that it could not be confirmed that supernatural apparitions were occurring there', though they did not say that they were definitely not occurring. Official pilgrimages to Medjugorje were forbidden, that is to say if they were led by clergy. Explaining this, Pope John Paul's Press spokesperson, Dr Joaquin Navarro-Valls, speaking to the Catholic News Service on 21 August 1996, said: 'You cannot say people cannot go there until it has been proven false. This has not been said, so anyone can go if they want.' He also said that 'the Church does not forbid priests to accompany lay-organised trips to Medjugorje.' The Church does not want to risk being tricked, but it does want genuine phenomena to be able to flourish. The only way this can happen is for Church authorities to keep a watch on such matters and step in in cases where things appear to be going wrong. After sixteen years of apparitions at Medjugorje, and more than twenty million pilgrims visiting, the Church has not intervened to prevent devotions, to censor teaching, or to caution clergy. The conclusion must be a presumption of 'sound tree' because no 'bad fruit', but the CDF has so far made no pronouncement.

There is no doubt that most Catholic Church leaders have been reluctant to take up what contemporary prophets offer in confirmation of Scripture and in guidance for a perplexed world. While any serious Catholic must appreciate the problem for the Church and its leaders of not being able to go out on a limb by giving approval to the claims of people who have not been thoroughly tested theologically, scripturally and by time, there is still a serious problem of conscience for the people touched by the phenomena. The reaction expressed is frequently that these are not matters of importance, and in some cases little attention appears to be given to what the contemporary prophets are saying about specific spiritual problems of our times. Too often the prophets who seek to awaken the Church and the faithful are sidelined, and kept waiting for responses to appeals, or are ignored or criticised by leaders who fail to lead. It may be harsh here to quote Isaiah 'Do not prophesy the truth to us ... take the Holy One out of our sight ...' (Is 30: 10–11), but the scepticism of the leaders ill-befits believers in a supernatural religion, one which every day asserts the miracle of the Eucharist on its altars. There is also a lack of sensitivity among those who comment adversely without taking to heart the concerns of the faithful or, which is much more serious, without seeming to acknowledge the mercy of God and the love of the Virgin Mary that has been expended even in those apparitions and messages which have been fully approved by the Church in the past, such as Guadalupe and Fatima.

7

Appeals and signs from Heaven

Apocalyptic private revelations

> *As it was in Noah's day, so it will be when the Son of Man comes. For in those days before the Flood people were eating, drinking, taking wives, taking husbands, right up to the day Noah went into the ark, and they suspected nothing until the Flood came and swept all away.* *(Mt 24:37–39)*

Although an irrational and suspect millennialism is held to account for widespread apocalyptic warnings in our time (Thompson, 1996), there has in fact been a tradition of modern apocalyptic thinking in Catholic consciousness for at least 150 years, since the Marian apparitions in Paris at the Rue du Bac, and in the Alpine village of La Salette. Such thinking was greatly intensified by the better known apparitions at Fatima in 1917 and by the way in which subsequent events, including the fall of Communism, both fulfil the prophecies of Fatima and prepare the ground for later prophetic messages with a strong note of urgency about the need for the world to change and to return to God. But the most important, and little acknowledged fact about these apocalyptic prophecies is that they are rigorously scriptural in their foundation, and are accepted in their general outline by the Church. The *Catechism* refers to Peter's first speech in Acts (Ac 2:17–21), and states:

> According to these promises, at the 'end times' the Lord's Spirit will renew the hearts of men, engraving a new law in

> them. He will gather together and reconcile the scattered and divided peoples. (CCC, 715)

The only uncertainty in Christian minds about the interpretation of such prophecies is the time to which they refer, but that was already the problem that Noah had to solve. The more recent private revelations referred to in this chapter affirm that humanity is now living through the end times in a literal, and not merely allegorical sense.

The first thing worth saying about contemporary end times prophecies is that there is a remarkable number of them. Canon René Laurentin, one of the world's foremost specialists in this area, has estimated that there are between two and three hundred separate claims of heavenly messages being received currently, and certainly in the thirty or so with which I have some familiarity the theme of 'end times' is emphatically present. It naturally follows that this book can only deal with a small proportion of the messages, and I have chosen to include those that have gained the greatest following and are the best known in the Catholic world of the West. There are several books which offer a more extensive, though panoramic sweep, and there are many sources for further information that I leave for the reader who wants to follow them up.[27]

To simplify the otherwise confusing task of referring to a number of different apparition sites and seers, each with a variety of messages, I have included most of the key elements on which I wish to comment in summary charts (see Fig. 1: Prophetic Appeals, p. 101, and Fig 2: Prophetic Signs, p. 106). In each chart, the different sites or messengers are taken from two of the three categories that were identified in Chapter Six, that is, private revelations that are officially approved by the Church, and those that are still awaiting Church discernment. It is noteworthy that the approved revelations are all historical, the most recent being Fatima, in 1917, which took thirteen years to receive approval. It is thus not surprising that there are many current alleged private revelations that are in the 'awaiting Church discernment' category. The prophetic messages given through the apparitions are divided into 'appeals' and 'signs'. The appeals are the main spiritual messages proclaimed by a particular seer, and intended as God's guidance in the trials of human life.

	Approved									**Awaiting discernment**					
	La Salette	Fatima	Sr Agnes	Ma. Esperanza	Kibeho	Fr Gobbi				2 Patricks	Christina	Medjugorje	Julia	Patricia	Renato
Appeals															
prayer/reparation	*	*	*	*	*	*				*	*	*	*	*	*
fasting/penance	*	*	*		*	*				*	*	*	*	*	*
Mass/Eucharist		*	*	*		*				*	*	*	*	*	*
rosary	*	*	*	*	*	*				*	*	*	*	*	*
confession				*	*	*					*	*		*	*
devotion to the two hearts		*	*							*	*	*		*	
consecration to Mary		*	*	*		*				*	*	*			*
peace/reconciliation		*		*	*	*					*	*		*	*
open to Holy Spirit				*		*					*	*		*	
seek Christian unity					*	*				*					
use of Scripture				*						*	*	*		*	
pray for Pope and priests			*			*				*	*	*	*	*	*
for souls in Purgatory						*						*		*	*

Figure 1: Prophetic appeals

The warning signs are those events in the world which are revealed or predicted by the seers, which may be either positive or negative in character. It is of course the negative signs, or predicted disasters, that have been inappropriately emphasised by sensation-seekers, and have frequently led to the neglect or misunderstanding of the purpose behind the appeals and warning signs as a whole.

It will be seen from the chart headings that there are six different apparitions or seers in each of the two categories of 'officially approved' and 'awaiting Church discernment'. There is little problem about the first category, since there is a fairly short list of such approved cases, and I have selected those which, unlike Lourdes for example, have an explicit link to the end times. Undoubtedly there will be some Catholics who will reproach me for giving consideration to not yet approved private revelations that they distrust, and others will say that I have missed out messages that they consider important. Regarding the private revelations 'awaiting Church discernment', I have had to make my selection on intuitive grounds, but the burden of the messages is in fact very similar to that of the 'approved' category. The stark warnings of the messages of Julia Kim, of Naju, Korea, and of Christina Gallagher, of Ireland, parallel those of Sr Agnes, of Akita, Japan, and the visionaries of Kibeho, Rwanda, while the global spiritual appeals of the messages of Medjugorje and of Fr Gobbi are similar to those of Fatima. Renato Baron, of Schio, Italy, and the two Patricks, from Ireland, are like Betania, with their emphasis upon the theme of love and the Eucharist, while Patricia, from London, is a special case, focussing almost entirely upon abortion, family issues and the mission to found a religious order. There are important additional cases, and I shall refer to some of these in the text. I do not think that their inclusion in the charts would change the general pattern of my observations or conclusions, but it would make the task of illustrating and comparing more difficult to achieve. [28]

Prophetic appeals

> *... store up treasures for yourselves in heaven, where neither moth nor woodworms destroy them and thieves cannot break in and steal. For where your treasure is, there will your heart be also.* (Mt 6:19–21)

The spiritual appeals in the messages are emphatically their most important element. Essentially they are a call to conversion to God and to a spiritual way of life, but one that is renewed by faith in God, hope in his promise of salvation, and love for God and neighbour. The main appeals are thus for prayer, fasting and penance to make reparation for sin, and the practice of a regular Catholic life of Mass and the sacraments, devotion to Jesus and to Mary, and work for peace and reconciliation, in personal lives, in society, and to resolve divisions in the Christian churches. These are the appeals which are common to nearly all the messages from the various private revelations.

* The least surprising observation is that prayer is the absolutely universal appeal in these messages. It may be worth stating the obvious here that the notion that the creature is invited to enter into a relationship with the Creator, a relationship to be sustained by the conversation of prayer, is fundamental to the Old and New Testaments, to the lives of the saints, and to the communal and liturgical life of the Church. It is above all through prayer that treasure is stored up in heaven.
* Less expected, perhaps, is the emphasis on fasting and penance, or the restoration of practices of self-denial that had been suspended in Church discipline in modern times. However, this is so strongly stressed in the messages of Medjugorje and those of the mystic and stigmatist Christina Gallagher (Petrisko, 1995) that it cannot be neglected.
* Similarly, the stress on praying the rosary, said by the Blessed Virgin to be the best defence against Satan, as well as upon regular confession, above all at Medjugorje which has been called the confessional of the world, challenges recent practice amongst many Catholics.
* The Virgin revealed at Fatima that God wished her to be venerated under the title of the Immaculate Heart, which represents her purity, her love, and her motherly awareness of her spiritual children. Mary is known by many titles, and often wishes to associate a particular apparition with one of these, for example at Lourdes, the Immaculate Conception, at Medjugorje, the Queen of Peace, and at Schio, the Queen of Love. The identity she thus assumed at Fatima was the Immaculate Heart.[29]
* Mary's heart is closely identified with the heart of Jesus, and in several sets of messages she reveals the importance of devotion to these two hearts, which are in fact inseparable because of their mutual love. Many saints, and above all St Louis Marie de Montfort, have practised this devotion, to the point of a personal consecration to the heart of Jesus through the heart of Mary, that is, identifying with Mary's own love and adoration of her divine Son.[30]
* Among the other appeals mentioned in the chart which are

points of emphasis in several messages is that for peace, the willing acceptance of God's will for oneself and for the world. At Medjugorje this theme of peace has been the dominant one. Related to this is the particular peace God desires for the Church, namely its unity.

* Some of the messages speak insistently about the need to give greater, and in fact daily attention to the living word of Scripture, through which it is possible to learn about God and to come closer to him. This emphasis is of special relevance to the Catholic laity, who are currently experiencing a great growth of interest in Scripture.
* Many messages speak of the role of the Holy Spirit in opening the way to personal holiness and in bringing about spiritual renewal in our times.
* Many call on believers not to forget those who have died, but who still need purification on account of their sins before they can enter heaven. The prayers of the faithful can help them by applying merit earned on earth to their cause, thus accelerating their purging. It is common Catholic practice to offer Mass for the dead, and these messages commend such prayers as well as other spiritual acts of mercy to the benefit of souls in Purgatory.
* The messages are often extremely pressing. Response to them is seen as urgent. In Fr Gobbi's messages there is a message to the 'apostles of the last times' in which they are requested to undertake the second evangelisation, proclaiming Jesus and his Gospel in the countries which were once Christian but have abandoned the faith. The priests, to whom these messages are especially addressed, are to be ministers of grace (through the sacraments) and of merciful love, announcing the return of Jesus in glory.
* The two Patricks speak above all of God's love for humanity, and of the need to offer a return of love, which their messages refer to as a 'revolution of love'. The way to this is through the same spiritual practices as are identified by the other seers, with prayer in the first place. Many of the other messages contain this appeal for love, including Christina's, Julia's, and those of Medjugorje and Schio.[31]

There is no doubt that these spiritual appeals are very

The spiritual appeals of the Medjugorje messages

- attend daily Mass (30 March 1984)
- offer three hours of prayer a day (4 July 1983)
- pray three rosaries each day (14 August 1984) as well as 7 Paters, Aves and Glorias for peace
- go to monthly confession (6 August 1982)
- give time for adoration of the Blessed Sacrament (15 March 1984)
- read the Scriptures daily (18 October 1984)
- pray before the cross (12 September 1985)
- observe family prayer (20 October 1983)
- make an act of consecration to the Sacred Heart of Jesus and to the Immaculate Heart of Mary (25 October 1988)
- undertake pilgrimages, penance, sacrifices, and fast on bread and water twice a week (27 June 1981)

demanding, even for the most convinced believer. When the Medjugorje apparitions first began in 1981, no Catholic pastor would have dared to ask from his congregation what Mary has asked in her messages. And yet many pilgrims returning from Medjugorje are now living them faithfully, week in, week out. How has this happened? It is this transformation that is the miracle of Medjugorje. It began among the local people. I still remember my sense of shock at seeing so many people in church for two and a half hours on a very cold January night in 1984; I recall the reverence on their faces, their gentleness, the rosaries I heard prayed in the fields, and in homes in the evenings, the queues for confession, and the example of fasting. I do not say that all the villagers lived like this, or that all do now, but I saw it and knew that it could be lived, and since then I have seen this way of life, this spiritual rule, spread like wildfire, as people all over the world have imitated them.

Prophetic signs

When these things begin to take place, stand erect, hold your heads high, because your liberation is near at hand.

(Lk 21:28)

	Approved									Awaiting discernment					
	La Salette	Fatima	Akita	Betania	Kibeho	Fr Gobbi				2 Patricks	Christina	Medjugorje	Naju	Patricia	Schio
Signs															
apostasy/heresy	*		*			*				*	*		*		*
rebellion in Church	*		*	*		*				*	*		*	*	*
attacks on priests			*	*		*				*	*		*		
Church persecuted	*	*	*			*				*					
Church Freemasonry						*				*	*		*		
antichrist coming	*					*				*	*				*
schism in Church						*									
plagues/Aids	*					*									
worldwide warning				*		*				*	*				
(3 days of) darkness					*	*				*	*	*			
chastisement	*	*	*	*	*	*				*	*	*	*		*
abortion condemned						*				*	*	*	*	*	
Marian dogmas	*		*	*		*							*		
millennial element					*	*					*				
new Pentecost						*				*					*
new era	*	*		*		*				*					*

Figure 2: Prophetic signs

The prophecies concerning the signs of the times refer both to the life of the Church and to the wider secular world. It was foretold at La Salette that the Church would experience heresy and apostasy, that there would be an antichrist, plagues and chastisement before a new era could be instituted by God.

A) Concerning the Church:

* Among the best supported of the contemporary prophecies concerning such signs of the end times from Catholic

sources are those that refer to God's allowing Satan to test the Church during the twentieth century. This was confirmed by the Blessed Virgin Mary to Mirjana, one of the Medjugorje visionaries, as having been revealed to Pope Leo XIII in the 1880's.[33] It is well known amongst Catholics that Pope Leo ordered that a special prayer of protection against Satan should be offered to the Archangel Michael after every Mass, and this continued for three-quarters of a century.

* It was thirty years later when the Virgin Mary at Fatima gave the three visionaries a message about the future that has never been made public. However, it is generally assumed that this message warned of divisions and a loss of faith in the Church, and now there is a whole range of prophets who refer to such issues in great detail.
* The most comprehensive predictions concerning prophetic signs are given in the copious messages of Fr Gobbi.[34] Grave problems for the Church arising from internal conflict are predicted, many of which had already been spoken of in earlier Church approved private revelations or have been repeated by other contemporary prophets, as can be seen from the second chart.
* There are predictions of widespread apostasy and rebellion by bishops, priests and theologians, and some seers foretell a schism in the Church and the coming of an antichrist, even of an antichrist usurping the Papacy as La Salette had warned. The antichrist is envisaged as a kind of vicar of Satan and a supporter of the idols of worldly corruption that give Satan his glory. In her messages, Christina Gallagher foresees the reign of an antichrist who achieves control over the governments and currencies of the world through the Maastricht treaty and the International Monetary Fund.
* Fr Gobbi's messages, as well as Christina's (Petrisko, 1995), affirm that we are living in the times of the Book of Revelation. His messages identify atheism, Freemasonry and ecclesiastical Freemasonry as the dragon and the two beasts of Revelation, chapters 12 and 13. The aim of these movements is the fulfilment of Daniel's prophecy of the 'disastrous abomination', that is, the taking over of the

Church by forces of evil (Fr Gobbi, message of 31 December 1992). The messages of the two Patricks speak of the danger to Pope John Paul II, and the usurping of his throne by the antichrist (message of 13 September 1996).[35] At the base of all these conflicts is the spiritual warfare waged by Satan on the Church, but his human agents are conspiratorial forces coordinated by Freemasonry which is seeking to undermine the Church from without and within. Besides Fr Gobbi's messages, this internal conflict is also plainly described by the two Patricks, Julia Kim in Korea and Sr Agnes of Akita (Flynn, 1993).

* There are related requests from nearly all the prophets to pray for priests who are subject to various kinds of temptation and corruption (Sr Agnes, Christina, Julia), and also to pray for the protection of the Pope whose ministry is the main bastion against moral and doctrinal collapse in the Church (Fr Gobbi, Christina, the two Patricks). These same divisions and rebellion in the Catholic Church, and the safeguarding of the Papacy from attacks from various external sources, were both foreseen in a famous dream of the nineteenth century Italian priest St John Bosco, in which the Church is saved by its devotion to Jesus and to Mary.

Many of these dire predictions are more plausible today than they would have been even ten years ago, and the reluctance in the 1960's of scholars like McKenzie to connect the Book of Revelation with modern times referred to earlier is therefore hardly surprising. Although there was a huge exodus from clerical and religious life in the later 1960's, there was not such a great degree of outspoken dissent as is manifest now. This has become so widespread that it is possible to speak of a general apostasy of the kind that is predicted in Scripture, foretold by the Virgin Mary at La Salette in 1846, and affirmed by many contemporary prophets. Apostasy is rarely called by its name, but John Paul II says in *Tertio Millennio Adveniente* (TMA):

> Faith, already put to the test by the challenges of our times, is sometimes disoriented by erroneous theological views, the spread of which is abetted by the crisis of obedience vis-à-vis the Church's Magisterium. (John Paul II, 1994, para 36)

B) Concerning the world:

* The non-believing world is also seen as sustaining an attack on the Church and its mission from the outside, leading to the persecution of priests and orthodox Christians, especially those loyal to the Eucharist, to Mary and the Pope (Fr Gobbi, Christina, Julia, and the two Patricks).
* For Christina, the greatest trial is the devil's onslaught on the priesthood, especially in Ireland. She calls for a response of the faithful by not judging priests, because no one can know to what attacks and temptations they are being subjected, and by praying constantly for them.
* Among the evils in the world that are most consistently condemned are abortion and other harm to children, sexual perversion, and above all the lack of a return of love to God.
* It is such evils, both inside and outside of the Church, that it is said will lead to a purificatory chastisement or correction, already visible in Aids as the first plague referred to in Revelation 16:2 (Fr Gobbi) and in other epidemics, natural disasters and wars, all of these being seen as the result of sin, and intended by God to bring people back to a true respect for his law (spoken of by Christina, as well as by Fr Gobbi and Sr Agnes). The messages of Patricia call for the Church to adopt the victims of abortion as martyrs, that is the innocents who have been massacred by a heartless society.
* We are told in Fr Gobbi's message of 15 September 1993, given in Japan twenty years after the apparitions in Akita ended, that its prophecies were now coming to fulfilment. A chastisement is foretold in which fire will come down from heaven and a great part of humanity will be destroyed (Sr Agnes and Fr Gobbi).
* The possibility of a third world war or of cosmic disasters, with the destruction of cities and even countries as an outcome of humanity's moral failure, figures in the messages of Julia. [36]
* The three days of darkness have been spoken of as a time when God will intervene to conclude the chastisement and turn everything around. The most recent detailed witnesses for this have been the American Franciscan friar, Br David Lopez, who received his message from the Virgin Mary in

Medjugorje, and was encouraged by his bishop to spread its details (Flynn, 1993), and the Spanish visionary, Luz Amparo Cuevas, of Escorial. There have long been prophesies that there will in the end times be three days of darkness, when the earth will undergo some major disaster, even to the extent of being rocked off its axis. One of the best known is that of Blessed Anna-Maria Taigi who in the last century said that this would be a time of purification during which no artificial light would function except that of blessed candles, and during which people should stay within their houses praying (Birch, 1996, p.362). There are contemporary prophets who say that they know nothing of this prophecy. For example, Christina Gallagher makes a point of saying that she has been given nothing on this subject, only that mankind has entered into 'a darkness' (which appears to be spiritual rather than physical). Without wishing to reject the notion of a specific trial of darkness, it is also true that the metaphor of darkness pervades the messages of the contemporary prophets. They speak of a darkness brought about by evil, a spiritual darkness of human error, sin, unlove and conflict, but a darkness that is often not perceptible to those affected by it. In a message of the two Patricks, England is said to be in darkness: 'Come back before the darkness becomes so black that no light will shine in it' (11 December 1994).

* Although the messages of Medjugorje have concentrated upon spiritual appeals, the visionaries say that they have been given secret messages about the future which include chastisements. These are to be revealed ten days in advance of their being fulfilled by the visionary Mirjana through a priest she has herself already chosen, Fr Petar Ljubicic, as confirmation that these events are intended as warnings to humanity.
* There are messages of hopefulness from most of the prophets. Contrasting with the threatened darkness we find also the metaphor of light, signifying clear vision, truth, goodness, love and harmony with God. At Medjugorje, the Blessed Virgin says, echoing the Gospel: 'You are the light of the world.' (25 October 1996).
* There is to be a new era in the world after these purifying

events have taken place. Indeed, this was the promise of La Salette in the middle of the nineteenth century. The triumph of the Immaculate Heart of Mary will, it is predicted, be the final factor that will usher in a new era of peace.

* It has been prophesied that a major dogma affirming Mary as Co-redemptrix, Advocate and Mediatrix of Grace is to be proclaimed at some stage in the course of these events (messages to Ida Perleman in Amsterdam). This case is interesting because the authenticity of these messages had long been disputed. However, on 31 May 1996, just days before Ida's death, the Bishop of Harlem authorised the cult of Our Lady of All Nations at the shrine developed around Ida's messages. Bishop Bommers did not pronounce on the messages themselves, but left this to the Church.
* The effect of the change of heart will be to bring about a spiritual renewal, a new Pentecost, in which people will return to faith in God and to a life of great virtue (message to Fr Gobbi, 21 November 1994).
* There is a considerable body of prophecy that anticipates a complete working out of the Almighty's plans by the year 2000, in what is fundamentally a cosmic struggle between good and evil, a spiritual war in which humanity is merely one of the elements. Thus in Fr Gobbi's messages there is a prophecy of Mary that her triumph will occur by the year 2000 (message of 5 December 1994). Several contemporary prophets have made essentially the same predictions, as it were staking their whole credibility on the almost immediate fulfilment of their prophecies (Christina). Yet at the moment, despite all the horrors of wars in various places, and highly publicised infidelities in the Church, there is calm, there is progress in proclaiming the truth, and the Church is held in esteem by many. It seems as if we are living in times when everything is at stake. Such ultimatums do occur quite frequently in Scripture, and were in some cases acted upon, on a local basis, as at Sodom. In preparing for such an eventuality believers must do more than seek to save themselves, because God wants the salvation of all. The Church will undergo its own crucifixion and be nearly, but never totally destroyed. Because the basic faith of Christians is in the resurrection,

there is always a reason to live positively, and in hope, and, as Scripture says, 'with heads held high'.

* There is a further aspect to the numerous apparitions which have been cited, and that is the fact that they are often reported as being accompanied by physical phenomena and signs which witnesses take as confirming their authenticity. It may be that this is the most difficult aspect of contemporary prophecy for modern readers to credit, and yet in Scripture the works of God were always accompanied by signs and wonders, even in apostolic times. The most famous sign of this kind was the spinning of the sun that occurred on 13 October 1917 on the day of the final apparition at Fatima. According to contemporary witnesses, this phenomenon was seen by 50,000 people who were present or in the vicinity, and the secularist newspaper, *O Seculo*, published a report acknowledging what had happened. Such events have become almost daily occurrences at Medjugorje and at some other apparition sites, including Kibeho. However, many other visible signs have been reported elsewhere, for example, a bleeding host at Betania, perfumes at Schio, statues of the Virgin Mary weeping at Akita and Naju, as well as the famous statue of the Virgin from Medjugorje that weeps at Civitavecchia in Italy, and rosaries' links suddenly changing to a gold colour. Mirna, the Greek Catholic visionary in Damascus exudes pure oil from her hands and has received the stigmata, or wounds of Christ, as have other visionaries including Julia, Christina, and Luz Amparo.

Phenomena of this kind have been consistently reported by pilgrims, often by bishops and other clergy associated with the visionaries and by scholars like Laurentin, and they are far too frequent and public to be disregarded.[37] It is also worth noting that the apparitions of Fatima and Medjugorje are mysteriously linked by the promise of an authenticating sign. At Fatima it was the spinning sun at the last apparition. And at Medjugorje it is to be a permanent sign at the site of the first apparitions on Podbrdo hill. Regardless of this link, or possibly confirming it, many had perceived the apparitions in Medjugorje to be a continuation of Fatima in its main messages.

Convergence of end times prophecies

> *So stay awake, because you do not know when the master of the house is coming, evening, midnight, cockcrow, dawn; if he comes unexpectedly, he must not find you asleep. And what I say to you I say to all: Stay awake.* (Mk 13:35–37)

A remarkable feature of the charts of prophetic appeals and signs that will not, I am sure, have escaped the reader's attention, is that there is such a pattern of convergence between these private revelations, which are among those most esteemed by the Catholic faithful, and which have the greatest following from various countries whether or not they have yet received official Church approval. First of all, the very fact that we are being appealed to for spiritual change and that we are being warned about future events implies, first, that we can respond, and do something about them, or at least that we can stay awake and prepare for them, and second, that the foreseen events are not unconditional, since we are being asked to pray for protection from them. Several times at Medjugorje the Blessed Virgin has spoken of these times as a time of grace. This means that this is still the time of God's mercy, when we can hope for a reversal of the trend of events, and for our salvation and that of others. However, the most sobering conclusion to be drawn is that the situation is urgent, that there is little time to delay or to risk not being ready. This view, in a sense, is obvious as it is more than justified by the state of the world which even total sceptics can acknowledge.

We could consider the almost total unanimity of the contemporary prophets as to the importance of the spiritual response. This is undoubtedly the principal feature of the apparitions and messages, though it is very difficult to ensure that this is heard as their most urgent message. Fundamentally, this is exactly what we learn from reading the Gospel. We are asked to follow Christ, the way, the truth and the life. In that sense we do not have to stake our lives on particular private revelations, but simply have to acknowledge how they point us back to the Gospel and its lessons about the way to a new and more abundant life. The elements of this life are those selected from the messages as having the greatest frequency of mentions, and they are the everyday practices of the Christian life, especially as taught by the Catholic Church.

The warning signs that are prophesied are to be seen as incentives to take the spiritual messages seriously, and the Blessed Virgin says now is the time, and not some time in the future when we have become convinced that Heaven really does want to be heard because we will have begun by then to suffer for our hardness of heart. Therefore, we hardly need to worry whether a particular prophet is authentic, since they virtually all say the same thing, whether formally approved by the Church or still awaiting its discernment. Whether we look at the Church or at the secular world they show us that there is a moral and spiritual collapse. The more we reflect upon the situation around us, the more we can see the godless void, the inversion of the hierarchy of creature and Creator, and the threatening signs of retribution stemming from our own evil use of each other and our ravaging of the natural order. If that situation leaves us indifferent, then we can turn our minds and hearts away from the Gospel, but if it makes us feel uneasy, then our conscience is evidently stirring us to respond.

The first reaction of anyone hearing these messages is to look for any evidence that they might be being confirmed in reality. Failing that, the situation remains uncertain, and uncertainty is embarrassing, so the whole subject becomes a taboo, especially among clergy, intellectuals and scholars. No one really wants to be found talking about it. The more plausible response is scepticism, or even fear of being swept along by the overly zealous, caution about the danger of being influenced by sensations, or picking on any characteristic of contemporary prophets that could be used to justify incredulity. I have encountered these reactions personally, and they might easily have stopped me writing this book, but instead the conclusion I have drawn is that there is enough evidence that the highly consistent messages of the contemporary prophets are the authentic voice of Heaven. I accept that we should not be avid for prophecy but rather live in trust in the Gospel. However, if we are given signs and guidance to help us, we should not neglect them. The problem for a

Christian believer is to keep everything in balance through faith, hope and love. It is not immature to find consolation in signs and prophecies, and mature to deny them. But it is immature to imagine that we can control God, and to summarily reject the mercy shown in his appeals and signs, as if creation belonged first to humanity and then, by some kind of human dispensation, to God.

Do we not have to admit, on reflection, that the situation in the world is not what we would have predicted thirty years ago? There is far more doubt about our future, far more moral precariousness, far less hopefulness about our relationships, our personal significance and our survival. Added to this we have the certain fact that the chaos of Kibeho and of Bosnia were both predicted by the Blessed Virgin long before they occurred. The visionaries in Africa saw headless bodies floating in the river years before the civil war made this a reality on our television screens. I have had books containing these prophecies on my shelves for years, but did not understand their connection to the future of the country from which they had emerged. Likewise, in Bosnia, Mary called for peace and reconciliation the very first time she spoke to the visionaries, and that turned out to be ten years to the day before the war broke out in their country.[38] Unless we are waiting for God to intervene on a cosmic scale before we will believe, how much self-induced human disaster is needed before we will decide that it is time to respond to Heaven's warnings?

I believe that many people are hoping for a clear and indisputable sign, and if and when it comes they will heave a sigh of relief and respond far more wholeheartedly than the way they currently take up their worldly tasks. What could such a sign be? One specific prophecy about the conclusion of these end times is of a worldwide warning about the moral evil in each soul, in which everyone will know that there is a God, and will see their soul as God sees it. The effect of this will be to give people a last incentive to decide for God, though still not under compulsion (Fr Gobbi, message of 22 May 1988, and several other private revelations; cf. Flynn, 1993).[39] If this single prophecy is borne out it could change the world overnight. The churches could be full of people seeking God, and wanting to learn from believers. Rather than the discouragement of the marginalised Christians, we would see the desperation of the would-be Christians. The obvious point is that these messages are not fundamentally for the unbelievers, but to incite the believers to ready themselves for the promised new evangelisation.

Mercy or justice?

> *I know the plans I have in mind for you ... plans for peace, not disaster, reserving a future full of hope for you.* (Jr 29:11)

It is none the less troubling that so many different calamitous events and outcomes are being prophesied. Even in the limited selection of private revelations included here, there are warnings of cosmic disasters, including the three days of darkness, natural catastrophes such as epidemics, floods and famines, as well as multiple wars, with possibly a nuclear conflagration. Then there are prophecies about Freemasonry gaining control of the Church and of world government, and of persecutions against the Church and especially priests, with the development of a schism in the Church. And finally, there are indications of direct acts of God outside of human understanding or the natural order. Taken all together, this seems excessive, if for no other reason that it would involve severe overkill. This therefore leads us to pose certain questions, at least to ourselves, in the hope of arriving, if not at answers than at least at some clearer view of what is at stake.

First, who would be the victims of the disasters: the sinners or the faithful? It could be the sinners, as in Noah's time, or it could be the faithful suffering with Jesus on the cross for the redemption of sinners. Secondly, what would be the intention of God in allowing such events to occur? Again, is it to let sinners suffer the consequences of their own evil, or is it to ensure the purification of the Church and of the faithful? Thirdly, at whom are the prophecies mainly aimed? Is it the evil conspirators, the individual sinner, Church leaders or the faithful? And fourthly, could some of the predicted events be different ways of seeing the same thing? For example, the three days of darkness might occur as the result of nuclear war or of a comet striking the earth, with any of these being able to provoke famine, flood and disease. A quite different possibility is to take seriously the warnings that Satan is conducting spiritual warfare against the Church by means of human agents, that is secularists and Freemasons who might use disinformation and manipulation of false prophecies, the promotion of false ideologies such as eugenics, free-market capitalism and secular materialism, to deceive all who were not on their guard, for, as St Paul says, false teachings can deceive even the elect.

This amounts to suggesting that there are basically two families of causation that appear to be plausible: on the one hand, a general disintegration in the natural and political order, a reign of chaos under no control, but brought about by the compounding of human errors from the moral to the ecological, and, on the other hand, a spiritual enterprise commanded by Satan, in which all the elements are part of a deliberate strategy that can only be foiled by spiritual means, that is by faith in God, prayer and penance, so that God intervenes decisively. Of these two possibilities it is the latter that makes most sense to the believing Christian. The hypothesis of a spiritual warfare that is being played out intensely in our time may strike non-believers as fanciful or even absurd, but Scripture clearly reveals the existence of a power of evil, and this scenario is the logical extension of all that we know of that figure from the revelation of Scripture and the tradition of the Church through its saints and the experience of exorcists.[40] The fate of the Church is undoubtedly linked with Jesus' life on earth: persecution, false accusations, victimisation by worldly powers, condemnation, crucifixion and resurrection. Thus, that innocent people suffer during their life on earth is entirely comprehensible to Christian faith. Likewise, as a counterpart to this suffering, there could be a just punishment for the guilty through the destruction of the worldly powers, just as Babylon is destroyed so that the new Jerusalem can arise. We cannot therefore escape persecution and purification if we want to be faithful to Christ, nor punishment, if we are willing to betray or deny him.

If we put all this together, not deliberately seeking the sensational, but objectively recognising the sinful state of the world and assuming the displeasure of God and the consequent concern of the Virgin Mary, and relying especially upon the unimpeachable apparitions of Fatima and the similarly sound messages of Medjugorje, we can see that many are already in rebellion or are being misled in the faith, and that grave spiritual and other consequences could result. We are given warnings about the way the world is going, and the approach of a time when the Lord will change the character of his actions from mercy to justice. Some of these warnings are alarming in a worldly or material sense too, since they refer to human and natural catastrophes. Yet, the messages also tell us that we do not need to be doom-laden, since we have a merciful God who is our Father and who loves us. His eventual plans are for our peace, even if we have to endure a time of correction. In this situation, how is the faithful Christian to respond?

The following chapters are an attempt to answer this question, but before leaving the theme of end times it is important to recognise the prophetic messages for what they are: reminders of what we already know from Scripture of our mortality, of God's disposition to mercy, of the inevitability of judgement and the possibility of damnation, and of the fact that because we 'do not know the day nor the hour' we are constantly, as it were, in the end times. The result of any changes that come about through a direct intervention of God's justice will be the restoration of God's order, his peace and his glory, and an era of peace for humanity in which all will recognise God and be united with each other.

It is a remarkable fact that the spiritual priorities and many of the prophetic signs on which contemporary prophetic messages are agreed are also to be found expressed in the works and speeches of John Paul II. The Pope is devoted to the Blessed Virgin Mary, and believes that it was she who saved his life when he was shot on the anniversary of the first Fatima apparition. He endorses Fatima and its messages. It is said by many who have spoken to him about Medjugorje that he supports it, and would like to go there. He constantly prays the rosary. He has consecrated himself to the Immaculate Heart of Mary and speaks of the devotion to the two hearts. He has also encouraged the cause for canonisation of Sr Faustina Kowalska, the nun from his former Polish diocese who died in 1937, and whose private revelations on the mercy of Jesus parallel so many of these later messages. In fact it could easily be shown from his writings that Pope John Paul endorses all the prophetic appeals shown in Figure 1. As for the warning signs, he is on record as warning about divisions in the Church, and his enthusiasm for the 2000 year Jubilee has certainly something of the prophetic about it. He evidently hopes for significant progress on Christian unity by that date, and perhaps for much more. But, more broadly, John Paul II is a man of enormous prophetic gifts. His role in world affairs has been that of a prophet, calling the world to take seriously the call of God, the issue of sin, including social or structural sin, and the ethical challenges of what he has termed 'the culture of death'. These qualities of Pope John Paul are probably most succinctly grasped by a perusal of the extended interview he gave to Vittorio Messori in *Crossing the Threshold of Hope* (John Paul II, 1994).

The Pope speaks continually of the need for a 'second evangelisation' of those nations which were once Christian but are no longer so. The biblical prophecy of the great apostasy, the widespread loss of faith, is now being fulfilled in the world. It has never been like this since the first spreading of the Gospel. This is a unique and distinctive historical moment. The Book of Revelation and history converge, and are further confirmed by papal teaching and the contemporary prophets. We cannot put dates on future events. It is not for us to attempt to guess how the Lord will act or what is in store for us – and that is certainly not the intention of this work. God's ways are not our ways, and we cannot reason out what he might do. What we can definitely say, however, is that all this calls for a prudent attitude towards the messages we are given, at least by accepting their invitation to faith and to a renewal of our spiritual lives. We can all understand this in our hearts. If we do not respond, then it is our personal responsibility. But, similarly, if we do not tell others what we have learnt, then we are contributing to their ignorance and potential downfall. God will warn us, and he will give us signs and miracles, but this will not be enough to bring everyone to conversion. God therefore wants all believers to be evangelists, to make known to everyone the good news and the warnings of the Gospel.

If I question myself about my own purposes in writing this book, I must admit that I am trying to advance the most plausible face of contemporary prophecy. I would like to make it as convincing as possible to sceptics. But that presupposes that I do believe in it, even in some of its apparently less plausible forms. On the other hand, no messages are just apocalyptic; they include a judgement on our present lives and a call to reform that is always valid. I thus conclude that we should respond to God's prophets prudently with repentance, prayer, and renewed faithfulness to his commandments and to his Church. If I learn from one prophet that the priorities are prayer, fasting, and love of God, and from others, humility, and Christian unity, there is little I can dissent from. If I hear from another that they are surrender, decreasing in self-importance and allowing God to increase, and the need for intercession for priests, I can agree to them without any violence to my conscience. If I then understand from a third that they are obedience to Our Lord and to Mary, and entrustment to them, I can readily see myself that I need such trust and the will to put God first always. It is possible that we may be mistaken in our interpretation of some of the signs, but at least we are never wrong in responding to the prophetic appeals.

There are however Catholics, and many other Christians, who suspect all contemporary or non-scriptural mystical or prophetic messages, alleging either that they come from the devil or that they are misguided in distracting the individuals concerned from the worship of God. It is therefore clear that this cannot be a mandatory and exclusive way for people to come to spiritual understanding. Evangelical religion, the charismatic movement, revivals, Bible fellowships, new Christian communities, prayer groups, and many other forms of conventional worship all contribute to spreading Christian faith and life. Many of these forms are actively used in the Catholic Church independently of the mystical way. The Gospel itself is the message. But whether people come directly to Scripture, or are led by the Church, or by the guidance of its saints, mystics and prophets, the common meeting point is the challenge not to remain in religious routines, still less in unbelief, and instead to accept a new life of the Spirit. This renewal is also evidence for the truth of Christ's teaching, and the best witness to unbelievers, as bringing about in a variety of different ways the response called for by the contemporary prophets.

8

Spiritual renewal

Grace and growth

I shall give you a new heart, and put a new spirit in you; I shall remove the heart of stone from your bodies and give you a heart of flesh instead. (Ezk 36:26)

Those who have accepted the utterances of the prophets, whether in scriptural or modern times, as coming from God, are consequently obliged to consider their implications for their own lives. The concluding chapters consider some of these implications. While there are many books on spirituality and devotions to which a reader can turn for information and help, the task here cannot be considered complete without some attempt to draw out of these specific prophetic teachings the experience and the lessons that apply to the spiritual journey that God desires everyone to take towards him. What God says is both old and new, the Gospel and the fulfilment of the Scriptures, on the one hand, and the Word incarnate preparing his second coming, once again through Mary and the Holy Spirit, on the other. He makes clear that he wants the renewal of the Church, the conversion of sinners and the bringing back to life and to truth of all who have strayed away. The prophets' task is to inspire us to believe, to love, to find a new life of peace in God by prayer, penance, and reconciliation. If we do not close our eyes and ears to God's speaking, we will understand in our hearts that he is coming, and that we need never doubt his mercy and his desire for our personal salvation, as Isaiah so vividly proclaimed. He is not a legalistic God requiring us to perform duties so that he can spare us from punishment. He loves us more than we can possibly imagine, and wishes to fill us with joy, love, and peace. For this to happen we only need to believe and give our assent.

Thus, he says to the two Patricks that he wants to rebuild his Church, that he wants us to work for the repairing of his house, just as he asked St Francis nearly eight centuries ago, and indeed the whole House of Jacob when he said:

> You will rebuild the ancient ruins, build up on the old foundations.
> You will be called 'breach-mender', 'restorer of ruined houses.'
> (Is 58:12)

The need is the same today. Only now there is a new note, the urgency of saving the faith when it is moribund, when so many who once were Christian have apostasised, and when many who claim to be Christian deny the supernatural, the miraculous, and the power of a God for whom, the Gospel tells us, 'nothing is impossible'. What is vital is the intimate link between God and his creatures. He is calling each one to conversion. He is not favouring his prophets and messengers. Indeed, their responsibility is especially great. What he says to them he is in effect saying to everyone. The messages are to be understood as addressed directly to whoever hears them.

The New Testament invites us to see our lives as a never ending opening up to new birth in the Holy Spirit; this was what Jesus won for us through his sacrifice on the cross, but it had already been prophesied long before, in Ezechiel: 'I will give you a new heart and put a new spirit in you' (Ezk 36:26). This new birth happens above all through baptism. The effect of the Spirit coming at baptism is to reveal the new Christian's true relationship to God. This spiritual rebirth, we are told, purifies us from sin which has separated us from God, and we receive forgiveness, and become sons and daughters of God (Rm 8:1–2). We are then called to grow, but through grace. A very significant feature of the *Catechism of the Catholic Church* is that it begins its section on morality, entitled 'Life in Christ', with the Beatitudes rather than the ten Commandments. The Law of the Old Testament is not being set aside; instead it is being completed by the New Testament which fully reveals the basic law of love as the summary of the Law and the Prophets. The implication of a spirituality based upon the Beatitudes is that our lives are seen as a search to express love, reflecting God's own love, rather than as an effort to match up to required norms of behaviour, as some might understand the notion of 'commandments'.

To those living according to their worldly desires, but in a spiritual coma, the Christian way of life may well be unwelcome. Some see it as obliging them to conform to a moral code, and so it appears restricting or rigid. Many therefore reject Christian morality as repressive, unjust or outmoded. But if, instead, we see living a Christian life as loving, relating, being supportive, positive, generous, or to quote St Paul, filling our minds

> ... with everything that is true, everything that is noble, everything that is good and pure, everything that we love and honour, and everything that can be thought virtuous or worthy of praise (Phil 4:8)

then we are not repressed, but have a possibility of being creative and adventurous about the way we follow Christ, bearing in mind that it is always the Spirit who inspires us. It is the same in all aspects of the spiritual life. We are not being corralled into a uniform state. We are not all asked to behave alike, according to prescribed rules. If that was the spiritual life, it would be enough for us to avoid backsliding without ever going anywhere. Instead, the spiritual life is a journey that leads us to God, a constant willingness to reach beyond ourselves under the effects of grace. It is an often repeated experience of climbing the foothills only to glimpse another range of hills beyond, a daily conversion from our limited view of good and evil, and a searching through our spiritual imaginations to grasp something more of God's goodness and his vision and plans for us in order to make a new act of commitment. This is no doubt why, in the eighteen months immediately preceding the time of writing, the Blessed Virgin's monthly messages from Medjugorje have used the word 'decide' or 'decision' no less than twelve times. In the spiritual realm it is always true that today has to be treated as the first day of the rest of our lives.

How the Holy Spirit helps

> *The Holy Spirit ... will teach you everything and remind you of all I have said to you.* (Jn 14:26)

It is most often in the Scriptures that those seeking God will find their first and clearest answer to their spiritual questions. The Scriptures are the word of God, and have an extraordinary power in speaking to human hearts, expressing the inexpressible in so many different ways, and meeting the needs of the individual soul. But there is a specific way in which this happens that is worth commenting on. We can read the Scriptures as though they were historical accounts, philosophical treatises, moral codes, love poems, or whatever analogy strikes us for a particular passage, but this is never all that they are. Scripture reflects a many-layered reality, the most obvious of which is very unlikely to be the truth that we are seeking. Frances Hogan, in her penetrating commentary on the Gospel of St John, illustrates beautifully how there is constantly a view from 'below' and a view from 'above' that characterises the gospel story (Hogan, 1988). There can of course be many belows and many aboves, but her essential point is that there is a natural and a supernatural level of understanding, and the latter is only achievable as a grace of the Holy Spirit. An example she cites is the conversation between Jesus and the Samaritan woman at the well in John, chapter 4. The woman conducts the conversation on the level of one who has to face the daily chore of drawing and carrying water and who, whether in simplicity or in irony, welcomes the thought of drinking the water that Jesus offers her, after which, he tells her, she will never be thirsty again. On another level, Jesus is speaking of helping the woman to see the truth, when he knows that her life is a confused mess with the current partner and five husbands she has had. At a still higher level Jesus is offering us all the complete answer to our spiritual thirst.

Catholics believe that they also have an inestimable help

towards their spiritual growth in the Eucharist. The concluding words of the Mass, often rendered as: 'Go in the peace of Christ, to love God and serve your neighbour!' are an invitation to be a Eucharistic people for the world. We have received, and now we give. We have understood, and now we teach. We have been healed, and now we heal others. We have been given life, and now we share life. We came to the Lord, and now he is sending us forth. We engage in a process of spiritual growth each time we come to and go from the Mass. The Mass must change us! When we find a new grace of prayer, a new opportunity for conversion, a new understanding of morality, a better sense of Christian priorities, new insights into the Scriptures, new associations with people in the Church, and so forth, this is evidence that we are being led along the way to God.

This renewal of spirit takes us closer to God, rather than being satisfied with keeping promises and standards. This is not to encourage spiritual vanity, but to allow us to see that God wants not only that we grow up, and grow older in ordinary maturity and wisdom, but that we become more holy, more wise with his wisdom and more filled with the gifts of his Holy Spirit, more trusting in him, more convinced of the truths of the Gospel, and more able to help others in their spiritual journey to God. This is also what the Blessed Virgin Mary stresses in so many of her messages. She asks us to allow God to change us; we cannot change ourselves. She wants us to be more fervent, to come to renewal and conversion, and thus to prepare ourselves to help renew the world. In so many ways she is asking us to be ready to grow spiritually through a more willing response to her call to open ourselves to God, who will change us through his Holy Spirit.[41]

A call to total conversion

Your mind must be renewed by a spiritual revolution ...

(Ep 3:23)

God created a perfect world, a world of natural beauty, harmony and order. The sins of humanity have disrupted this

How the Holy Spirit changes us, according to Scripture

- we learn to see our lives afresh (Jn 3: 5)
- we come to understand Scripture through the light he gives us. (Ep 1:17–18)
- the Holy Spirit helps us to become more like God, to become holy (2 Co 3:18)
- the Mass, and our whole spiritual life is transformed (Ep 3), so that we sense a greater intimacy in our relationship to God, and a growing desire for prayer
- we receive the fruits of the Spirit (Ga 5:22–23)
- we receive a variety of gifts, including prophecy (1 Co 12:7–11), for the benefit of the Church
- we can be filled with the Spirit (Ep 5:18), so that the Spirit guides us in our lives 'Since the Spirit is our life, let us be guided by the Spirit ' (Ga 5).
- the Holy Spirit calls us into one body, unites us and energises us spiritually (1 Co 12:13)
- teaches us everything (Jn 14: 26)
- leads us to the complete truth (Jn 16: 13)
- guides us through our consciences and helps us to pray (Rom 8)

order but, according to the prophets, only temporarily. God intends that this disorder will end. He has in fact already taken the measures necessary to restore peace and order to the world by sending his Son, Jesus, who showed God's true nature on earth: his love, compassion, forgiveness, and his justice. God does not hide his designs. The problem is rather to understand why God, despite his disapproval of human sinfulness, relents and does not put things right without delay. We see humanity destroying itself, with people dragging each other into 'disaster, degeneration and war' (the prayer of Ida of Amsterdam). We also see what he has done, in the life, death and resurrection of Jesus, but we want an immediate solution to human ills. We want to see God's plan working out, but he is patiently waiting for the conversion of hearts.

We are called to love, then, because he loved us first (1 Jn 4:19). However, this same passage continues:

> Anyone who says 'I love God' and hates his brother is a liar, since a man who does not love the brother that he can see cannot love God whom he has never seen. So this is the commandment that he has given us, that anyone who loves God must also love his brother.' (vv. 20–21)

This could be a key to the whole of Scripture and of the spiritual life, of renewal and of finding our way in the darkness of sin and unbelief. If I can realise that everything that I see in creation, all that I have received, everybody I have cared for or who has cared for me, is all evidence of God's love penetrating through the materiality and otherness of the world to reassure me of the unique, powerful, direct and incontrovertible truth that God loves me, this can be my starting point for a new existence; it is the reality of eternal life. To know God truly is to know that I am loved. God is a God of mercy and love. He has been infinitely patient with us, but he greatly desires a return of love. We need to understand that he has loved us when we did not know him, when we did not love him, when we rebelled against him, and also of course when we were seeking him. Therefore he will not turn away from us if our hearts are sincere, even if we still are unable to recognise him. Faith is in his gift, and it is enough that we desire it to be on the good path.

I never fail to be amazed at the route my own life followed. First I thought that I had faith, and I lived as one who was secure and certain. Then it seemingly evaporated and I was in spiritual darkness. Finally a new light dawned that was stronger than before, but with a certain wisdom about the fact that it is not enough to claim both faith and salvation in one gulp, as some born-again Christians seem to do. We win our salvation through Christ, but we keep it through our faithfulness and our active love in response to the promptings of the Holy Spirit, by living in a state of grace. This is not fideism, the theory that faith alone saves us, but holiness, the holding onto God and keeping him in our hearts. This sense of total conversion is captured for me by a few lines written by the poet John Bradburne, who died while looking after lepers in Zimbabwe in 1979:

> God's love within you is your native land
> So search none other, never more depart,
> for you are homeless save God keeps your heart.
> (quoted in Dove, 1983)

Before my return to the Church I had had a long exile. Much could be said about it, but the essence was coming to a fuller appreciation of some basic things of which I had always had only a very hazy idea. I was surprised to find that the religious commitment of middle age was not comparable to that of a young person. It was enormously enriched for me by the experience of growing up, marrying, and having a family and a job. But the search for meaning and purpose are universal, and it does appear that the journey out of spiritual exile is as much as anything a journey back, a return to innocence. It is much more a purification of the soul than an accumulation of new knowledge or a growth in human wisdom. It took me some time to realise what was happening, and to come to a sense of a new unity and purpose for my life in which I could see connections between the present and my childhood. A key notion for me at that time was that I could take responsibility for my own life, and not be paralysed by the sense that everything was decided for me, either by my parents long ago, or by the Church, or just by others surrounding me in life. What I can truly say however is that, from that day to this, by God's grace I have not wavered in my belief in the meaning and truth of the Gospel and the sacred tradition of the Church.

Coming to the Gospel with the new energy of heavenly encouragement demands living more intensely what is already known. This may apply at a personal level, requiring of us an ongoing conversion, a spiritual journey of renewal and of growth in holiness, or it may invite a particular response from the whole body of the Church. Out of continuous reflection upon all these sources of inspiration the Church arrives at moments when she asks God's people for something fresh, even a revolution of spiritual dimensions. This happened for the Catholic Church at the time of the Second Vatican Council, and the present time is once again a moment of great upheaval as members of the Church seek to discern what is needed in the world today. Are we able to recognise the opportunity of this time, and to seize it? For some, the need is for a greater alignment of the Church with the modernising tendencies of the secular world, leading to greater freedoms, welfare and equalities in human society in line with gospel precepts. For others it is a matter of coming closer to Jesus Christ spiritually in attitude and conduct, and thus to a higher degree of personal holiness. It is false to separate these two tendencies, since both are of the essence of Christianity; but a polarisation of theologies, attitudes and lifestyles has indeed occurred along these lines leading to a division in spiritualities in the setting of political and social priorities for the Church over against a choice of liturgical, prayer, and devotional emphases in the spiritual journey. What can be said is that whether the response is a personal or a collective one, the impact on secular society is essentially counter-cultural. Spiritual values do not endorse secular values; they undermine and relativise them.

Even if we claim that the Catholic Church really understands about the spiritual, can we take it for granted that all believers share this sense? One of my sociology professors used the phrase 'the routinisation of charisma' to indicate the way that Jesus has founded the Church with tremendous power, how Pentecost then expanded that power, driving it out into the world, and how then St Paul gathered, structured, and institutionalised the preaching of the good news to the nations, helping the Church to take an organised shape. This process was necessary for the Gospel to spread, but also posed a risk to its purity. A creative tension inevitably exists between the institutional and the spiritual. The spiritual needs the institutional to survive, but the institutional needs the spiritual even more. It is getting the balance that matters, and the routinisation of charisma is a characteristically sociological expression for the way that power can be tamed and its real strength denied by expressing it in terms of rules and labels. Ritual is not necessarily spiritual. It can be, but in itself is not necessarily so, unless it also has an inner meaning and a living dynamic.

Strengthening the spiritual within the Church means finding energy for renewal, for constant conversion. And it is that aliveness that counts, not fixed characteristics of the kind that encourage adversarial criticism, stereotyping and labelling.[42]

For example, some forms of liberation theology have encountered opposition in the Church, because they were seen as predominantly directed to building the earthly kingdom through an essentially political revolution. Pope John Paul II, on the other hand, has made it clear that, for him, while the most important liberation is liberation from sin, part of the liberation from sin is liberation from sinful social structures. This latter view has found official expression in the Church (Congregation for the Doctrine of the Faith, 1986). Conversely, some spiritual movements such as the charismatic renewal have been criticised for not putting sufficient emphasis upon the everyday world, and too much upon divine intervention.

A new Pentecost?

> *But when the Spirit of truth comes he will lead you to the complete truth ... and he will tell you of the things to come.*
> (Jn 16:13)

Despite the Pentecost story, and the extraordinary diffusion of the Gospel in the lifetime of the apostles, the Church in the West tended over the centuries to neglect the Holy Spirit, leaving him virtually to be rediscovered in our time. The perfect unity of the Trinity leads us to see its three persons in constant relationship, and indeed liturgical prayers normally end with an invocation to the Trinity. The Trinity provides the prototype for a communion of persons united in love that all are called to imitate. Our communion with each other is to reflect the communion of the Godhead 'in the unity of the Holy Spirit', and to open all believers' minds and hearts directly to God. Such love would not be possible without the inspiration and help of the Holy Spirit.

Although the Old Testament did not reveal either the Son or the Holy Spirit directly, there were hundreds of prophecies of the Son, and there are many intimations of the work of the Holy Spirit, beginning with Genesis, where we read that the Spirit of God hovered over the inchoate creation. Jesus speaks often of the Holy Spirit in the Gospels, but especially in John 14–16, where he promises the coming of the Holy

Spirit after his own glorification. It was as if the promise of the Holy Spirit was Jesus' testament, and Pentecost was the receiving of the bequest, when the activity of the Holy Spirit came into the open, visible to all, for the building the Church. At Pentecost, the Holy Spirit manifested himself as a strong wind, as tongues of fire, and as the light of a new understanding, all symbolising the strength of the Gospel that converted three thousand people that very day. Another example of the Holy Spirit coming in power in the New Testament is at Peter's visit to the house of Cornelius (Ac 10:44–46), when a group of unbaptised people are suddenly filled with the Holy Spirit. The Creed also affirms that the Holy Spirit 'spoke through the prophets'. It is the Holy Spirit who inspired Scripture, and it is through the power of the Holy Spirit that we can understand the meaning of Scripture. Teaching about the Holy Spirit has greatly developed in the Church in recent years, notably in *Lumen Gentium*, the Constitution on the Church of the Second Vatican Council, and in Pope John Paul's encyclical *Dominum et Vivificantem*. We can see more and more that, following the age of the Father in Old Testament times, and the age of Jesus in New Testament times, we are now living in the age of the Holy Spirit, possibly even in the times of Joel's prophecy cited earlier when the Spirit is to be poured out on all mankind.

One of the prophets to whom the text from Joel could well refer is Marthe Robin, the French mystic who died in 1981, and who predicted a 'new Pentecost of love', a time when the Church would be renewed by the Holy Spirit from within, by the spreading of divine love throughout a seemingly cold and at times lifeless institution (Ephraim Croissant, 1990, Chapter Five). She said that this renewal would be mainly the work of lay people. It would be true to say that Marthe herself is in some measure responsible for the signs that this new Pentecost is actually occurring. She came to know many of those who have been leaders of renewal movements in both lay and religious organisations, and several of them have attributed to her much of the inspiration for their work. Among them are Br Ephraim, founder of the Community of the Beatitudes and Fr Marie-Dominique Philippe, founder of the Congregation of St John (Philippe, 1994, Part 3, Chapter

Four). These two communities have given ample evidence of a new Pentecost by their success in attracting hundreds of young people to lives of religious consecration and in the rapid spread and outreach of their ministry to countries across the world.

The works of the Holy Spirit

> That very day about three thousand were added to their number ... The faithful all lived together and owned everything in common; they sold their goods and possessions and shared out the proceeds among themselves according to what each one needed. (Ac 2:41–45)

New spiritual, mainly lay communities have been established in great numbers over the past quarter of a century, especially in France. Characteristically, they bring together people with vows, priests and nuns, lay people, married and unmarried, families with children, sometimes living in community, sometimes merely associated with each other within a neighbourhood or town.[43] John Paul II has referred frequently to the importance of this development that is owed to the Holy Spirit. For example in a talk to European youth at Strasbourg in 1988 he referred to them as 'one of the surprising manifestations of the Holy Spirit in the Church today' He added that ' the new communities offer a promising sign.... Uniting the spiritual search and temporal action, they offer a Catholic synthesis'.

The Community of the Beatitudes, founded in France in 1975, is one with which I have had personal contact over many years. One of its houses, the Abbaye Blanche, developed new approaches to evangelisation, including using video or puppet shows to evangelise children, audiocassettes, writings, and street evangelism. Other houses have targeted particular groups such as the divorced or those hurt by abortion. Activities of this kind stem from an intense prayer life, featuring Eucharistic liturgy and adoration, and Marian devotion including the rosary, pilgrimages and retreats. The Community's liturgy especially is quite remarkable; it responds in many ways to Eastern Orthodox inspiration, as in its use of icons and incense, and it has introduced new musical forms with a spiritually creative tone. Such groups have found a way of making their spirituality attractive to young people. The Beatitudes communities, some with close to a hundred people of all ages, have a relatively youthful membership. They have plentiful recruits and are bringing people into community and religious life as nuns and priests. The keynote of such communities seems to be that they are free from many of the institutional attachments of the past, even though they are invariably linked to dioceses and subject to the local bishop, and they appear to be offering something new in the Church that is much needed and appreciated.

The new movements centre themselves upon the Holy Spirit to avoid compromise with the false prophets of marginally Christian and non-Christian spiritualities, many of which need to be challenged for their deceptions and harmfulness. Seemingly religious rewards have come to serve as idols in the theocratic states of Islam, the New Agers' age of Aquarius,[44] the kingdom on earth of the Jehovah's Witnesses, or the kingdom of justice and peace of those liberation theologians who forget the essential fact that our lives on earth last but for a day. Alternatives to religious faith have also never been so available: rewards of a material or political kind, the Zion of some of the Jews, a New World Order or One World Government advocated by leading politicians in the most industrialised countries, the capitalist versions of the faded visions of the victory of the master race, or a workers' state, and, more prosaically, the hedonism of drink and drugs, the alienation of a whole generation from formally established institutions and customs, secular humanist outlooks, escapist activities in music, sport, entertainment, sexual licence and consumerism, and above all the pursuit of wealth or simply of money. All these are ways in which people have allowed themselves to be side-tracked from authentic religious faith and practice. Added to this is the fact that the last thirty years have seen an acceleration of the spread of these tendencies throughout the world. Together they represent a spiritual crisis to which the new communities are part of a vital response, which is seen by some as the beginning of a wider return to religion,[45] and indeed even to the model presented by the life of the Church in apostolic times in Jerusalem.

Apart from the new communities, other spiritual developments inspired by the Holy Spirit occurring in the Catholic Church today include a revival of interest in spiritual retreats and in methods of meditation and prayer, the charismatic movement that has spread from Protestant Churches and renewed the spiritual lives of millions of Catholics, the reopening of ancient pilgrimage routes, the major new Marian apparition shrines and the interest in contemporary apparitions and prophecies, and the impact of an inspired and extremely outgoing leader at the head of the Catholic Church. The Church has always fostered spiritual development through the work of Church leaders, saints and innovators over the centuries who have played instrumental roles in spiritual renewal, but there is a current sense that we cannot simply return to the past in this area. We need to be open to what will be appropriate for a different kind of world, a world in which the distribution of the population is changing, the cultural contexts have evolved, and where therefore the spiritual needs are different. One major example is that the long held differences between Christian denominations that have characterised the second millennium now seem increasingly unacceptable, yet the route to Christian unity has still to be discovered.

One of the success stories of recent efforts at spiritual renewal in Britain has undoubtedly been the Alpha courses. This strategy for local evangelisation was developed within the Church of England, but is now being widely taken up across the spectrum of denominations, including in the Catholic Church. A series of well-structured short talks about the basic elements of Christian faith, linked to group sharing, with a meal as part of each evening's programme, seem both to lay the basis for a personal approach to faith and fellowship, and to offer a clearer emphasis upon an experience of personal conversion under the pastoral guidance of the Church than, for example, the traditional Catholic adult initiation rite. In particular, course members get some understanding of the centrality of the figure of Jesus, and how it is possible to have a truly personal relationship with him.

And while there are questions about some aspects of the content, which draws heavily upon the Evangelical tradition with its weak sense of Church, of the sacraments, of authority, and its neglect of Mary and the saints, these areas can be developed as desired in any particular programme.

Such experiences of renewal as we can observe in the Church today seem to make it clear that the preaching of the Gospel will never be achieved by planful organisation, or certainly not by this alone. The much more essential ingredient is divine love, the love of the Gospel, the love that Jesus asked his disciples to have for one another, and which can only be inspired by the Holy Spirit. The decade of the 1990's was proclaimed a decade of evangelisation, and this project was adopted by many Christian denominations. Apart from the Alpha courses and some scattered smaller initiatives, however, it is hard to find much evidence that the hopes expressed have been fulfilled. This does not imply that the inspiration was not genuine, but it must mean that the challenge has not been taken up in the spirit of the Gospel, but only as a human project. This is not yet the new Pentecost. It has to be remembered that the first Pentecost did not occur amongst totally unprepared individuals, but rather a group of disciples who had been through a gruelling spiritual formation over a period of three years in the daily company of Jesus. That formation was a grounding in the values and work of gospel ministry. The new Pentecost can only strike root where there is this same well-prepared soil. The Holy Spirit needs our willing preparation to be able to bring us the grace we need. But to be ready for the coming of the Spirit we have to offer our repentance and surrender. St Peter taught this to the people after Pentecost when, in response to his proclamation of Jesus as the Christ-Messiah, they asked him what they should do. He told them:

> You must repent, and every one of you must be baptised in the name of Jesus Christ for the forgiveness of your sins, and you will receive the gift of the Holy Spirit. (Ac 2:38)

The challenge to answer

The Spirit and the bride say come! (Rv 22:17)

It may be that in the past Catholics lacked this personal sense of Jesus because they relied so much on institutional forms of prayer, and that the new priorities of Vatican II left people needing to rediscover the transcendent, freed from stereotypes. It seems that there is a spiritual vacuum in this sense for many Catholics, and that the Church needs to find how to help them to fill it. There are insufficient formed spiritual guides, and a lack of balance in many current approaches, where some have taken on responsibilities for which they were not equipped. They need to learn, share and grow more through new kinds of formation, and the central importance of community-building needs to be addressed by the Church. The Church also needs to be informed about New Age spirituality and the mushrooming sects and cults, and to understand how young people especially find these options so attractive. It is important to be discerning about them before entering into dialogue, but without writing them off as wholly negative, especially where they present themselves as minority tendencies responding to prophetic or mystical experiences within Christianity.

Since Christianity is an incarnational faith, the world of flesh and blood matters, in itself and for salvation. Life on earth is finite, but it has infinite significance, because it is during life on earth that each of us works out our eternal salvation. Therefore, it is essential to live consciously, to see what spiritual decisions we are taking and why, what the implications of these decisions are, and how we are contributing to or diminishing the common good of humanity by the way we live. Thus, spiritual renewal affects our morality, ethics, relationships, and their outcomes in terms of justice, peace, love and human welfare. Frequently Christian faith and morality are reproached as if they betrayed humanity in their tenets and values, when instead they provide the only standpoint left by which Western culture can prise itself out of the morass of self-destructive values in which it is currently asphyxiating itself. Church teaching warns continually of the culture of death that has developed, by which human life is being eroded through abortion, eugenics, euthanasia, and the divorce of sexual functions from reproduction, and even from love. The contrast of scriptural and worldly images has become startling, a true spiritual crisis, all the worse for not being truly and honestly recognised. The greatest loss in contemporary utilitarianism is that of a sense of the human person as made in the image of God, intended by the Creator to find fulfilment in relationship with divinity and humanity, in inviolable dignity and with eternal spiritual value.

In his apostolic letter, *Tertio Millennio Adveniente*, issued to encourage spiritual preparation for the new Millennium, Pope John Paul has proposed a three year phase of prayerful renewal for the Church, with one year devoted to each of the members of the Holy Trinity (John Paul II, 1994). After a year devoted to Christ, the second year, 1998, focuses on 'a renewed appreciation of the presence and activity of the Spirit'. This should help to encourage a wider recognition of the revival of the gift of prophecy in the Church, especially as an 'agent of the new evangelisation' (para 45). The letter states that the evangelising work of the Church should be directed both internally and externally, with a strong commitment to Christian unity, and to a positive response to 'the signs of hope present in the last part of this century, even though they often remain hidden from our eyes' (para 46). This emphasis placed by the Pope on spiritual as opposed to secular signs of the times and on the advent of the new Millennium parallels closely the perspectives adopted by many of the contemporary prophets featured in the previous chapter. However cautiously he phrases his thoughts, it seems clear that Pope John Paul expects dramatic events to accompany humanity's arrival on the threshold of the Millennium. Moreover, his watchword is hope, and it is events favouring the Church and the preaching of the Gospel that he has in mind, particularly in relation to Christian unity (paras 34–35).

The new Pentecost can therefore be expected to be a universal manifestation of the Holy Spirit, not merely local religious revivals such as have occurred in the charismatic renewal movement in recent decades. Much more likely it will sweep across all the churches and unify denominations, and also embrace cultural, artistic and political life. The two Patricks speak in their messages of the need for a 'revolution of love'. This has a ring of authenticity, and it is not only disciples that need to become more committed, but a whole civilisation that needs to be spiritually renewed: its government, laws, customs and morals, as well as its intellectual and cultural life. When I spoke of a significant moment in Western culture in Chapter Two, I had in mind this opportunity for a movement of the Spirit which could renew even secular society, and certainly transform the Church. Will God begin to turn the tide of atheism? Will Christians once again find in themselves the power to recall everything Jesus said and to understand his truth and to dare to speak the Gospel to the world? Is this utopian thinking, or is it a biblical promise of a time of love and peace that has yet to find fulfilment? Perhaps this will bring Jesus' second coming substantially nearer, to answer the longing of the Church, the Bride inspired by the Holy Spirit (Rv 22: 17). The interpretation I place upon contemporary Catholic prophecy is that the Holy Spirit is soon going to bring about a new Pentecost, that this spiritual transformation is in God's plan for our times, and that we are already beginning to perceive how this can come about in our personal lives, in the Church and in the world.

9

The world is called to return to God

All must choose

> I set before you life or death, blessing or curse. Choose life . . . (Dt 30:19)

However satisfied some people may be at the present time with their own situations, power, wealth and luxuries, there is hardly anyone who will say that the world is in a good state, that goodness is honoured even in their consciences. There is a sense that we are getting away with something, that we should be very different, politicians, church leaders, business people, parents, youth, in short, nearly every conceivable category of people. Yet we seem to find no energy, values or principles for spiritual renewal. Is this situation one that can endure, or are we at a point of such crisis that a breakdown of society is becoming imaginable? If the situation is acknowledged to be serious and urgent, what can be done? If, as I have been suggesting all through this book, the situation is now catastrophic, *what can be done?* I believe that it would be shirking the task of this book to avoid facing this question, or at least posing it as a practical issue, not just for Christian believers but for all people of good will.

But, first, how do we make sense of the question, and of its many ramifications across society, economy, culture, politics and religion? These are the very concerns that are addressed by Scripture and by the contemporary prophets whose messages we have been examining. And they do provide an answer to our problems, but it is so radical that hardly anyone is ready to contemplate it in spite of the chaos we see around us. At the beginning of 1997, the Blessed Virgin gave a message through the Medjugorje visionaries that sums up both the problem and the solution. She says:

> Dear Children, I invite you to reflect about your future. You are creating a new world without God, with only your own strength, and that is why you are unsatisfied and without joy in your heart. This time is my time, and that is why, dear children, I invite you again to pray. When you find unity with God you will feel hunger for the word of God and your heart, dear children, will overflow with joy and you will witness God's love wherever you are.
>
> I bless you and I repeat to you that I am with you to help you. Thank you for having responded to my call. (25 January 1997)

The problem, according to this message, is that so many people have utterly rejected God, and have sought to construct a world in which he has no place. This is the error that has brought human society to its present impasse. The solution is nothing less than to turn to God, acknowledging our true helplessness and seeking God's help and Mary's intercession to change our world totally, to reinstall goodness, truth and love.

In a sense, all must choose, since not to choose to return to God is to choose the chaos that will ensue. To be able to make an authentic response to Mary's prophetic call we are in need of a spiritual vision which can focus our attention upon the truth taught definitively by Jesus in the Gospel. St Paul once told the Corinthians:

> ... we will have none of the reticence of those who are ashamed, no deceitfulness or watering down the word of God; but the way we commend ourselves to every human being with a conscience is by stating the truth openly in the sight of God. (2 Co 4:2)

In modern terms St Paul warns against exchanging any short-term materialistic objective for the ultimate meaning and purpose given to life by the Creator. This is not only a viewpoint but a way of life, that is, a firm commitment to the faith and hope given to us by the New Testament. This vision provides the principle of coherence for the philosophy, cultural reality, and the social and political order that could restore hope to modern societies. Sadly, the principal prophet of such a vision for Christianity in the world today is continually rejected and vilified. Pope John Paul II is often presented by the media as someone who harks back to a golden age of Christendom, but those who study his speeches and writings will appreciate that his vision does not imply a mere reliving of the past, and certainly not a theocratic regime. It is the case that in building the nations of today we must look to our foundations, including the foundations of Christian culture, but what we must be seeking is the expression for our own time of the timeless Christian faith, with all its mystery and transcendent power, not merely its rational and social convictions. Inevitably, in the West, this process is very close to a rediscovery of our Christian roots that can both take us back to the past of our spiritual memories and point us towards the future of our spiritual hopes, that is the promised paradise of the Book of Revelation.

This rediscovery is certainly as much about unlearning as learning. It is entirely understandable that people today find Christianity difficult to accept because the Christianity they know at second hand often reflects such an accretion of human obsessions and habits which obscure its truth and its essential nature. Paradoxically, the figure of Christ himself has been a difficulty, though this was of course foretold in Scripture: he would be a 'sign of contradiction' (Lk 2:34). No doubt opponents of Christianity have in part manufactured the image of a pathetic figure whose life was a failure, and whose apparent spiritual beauty was a tragedy of misunderstanding and missed opportunities. Jesus was first rejected by the Pharisees, and by all those who expected the Messiah to inaugurate an earthly kingdom, and later his divinity was rejected by Christian heretics, adherents of other faiths, and eventually by the secular rationalists of the modern era.

However, along the way, Christians have contributed to the false Jesus by their dreams and emotional needs. They helped to manufacture a Jesus who was anodyne and passive, anthropomorphised and emasculated by artists of much sentimentality, but insufficient faith to perceive the inner strength of Christ's love. Perhaps the current impact of icon painting on the West is a good example of how our artistic sensibilities can be renewed without being so modernised that we lose any link with the essential truth of their source. What is not invalidated is the truth to which artists and believers are responding. And it is this essential truth that endures, 'the One who was, who is and who is to come' (Rv 1:8). It would be tragic indeed if we were to miss the truth because of the particular expression of it, whether in artistic form or in the words of Church teaching. The beauty of the Gospels is always there, but many do not turn, as Mary asks, to the word of God, with its spiritual vivacity and consoling promises. If they did they would see that there is joy and hope for humanity, that whatever has gone wrong, either in their own lives or in the world, can be put right.

The fall of Babylon

> *The kings of the earth will say 'Mourn, mourn for this great city, Babylon, so powerful a city, doomed as you are within a single hour.'* (Rv 18:9–10)

A concern with the unfolding of a heavenly plan for the world is apparent throughout Scripture. As was mentioned earlier, the Jews have always believed in the lastingness of the promises recorded in Deuteronomy, when there would be a return from exile. This was seen as the Covenant that God had made with his chosen people. The same destiny belongs to the new Israel, the Church, except that the Christian Sion is not a geographical but a spiritual destination of which Jerusalem was a mere symbol. The promise conveyed by Moses to the Jews has not been abrogated, but it has rather been extended in two ways: to encompass a destiny in a new resurrected life won by Christ, and to apply this to the benefit of the whole of humanity. There are several confirmatory passages in the Gospels where the end of the world is pictured, when Christ will come in glory to give judgement, and when there will be an end to human existence in its present form. The Gospels are no less dramatic and even apocalyptic than any of the contemporary prophets. However, it is in the last book of the New Testament that these prophecies are expressed in a most graphic, albeit obscure way.

These final two chapters closely reflect the Book of Revelation, itself a synthesis of the story of the human race's journey out of exile. It is a journey that is inspired by a vision of faith without which there is no destination. This faith is the spiritual knowledge of 'the treasure hidden in the field ' that brings hope for the Kingdom of Heaven. Human life in its fullness reveals the rebirth and growth of a holiness that spreads out from individuals to the whole race through the spiritual community of the Church, the 'bride adorned for her husband', Christ. In his work, *Catholicism*, Henri de Lubac offers a marvellous vision of how important the Church is to this final outcome. Because God created the human race, not just individuals, the Church in some way precedes the individual believer, just as the race is more complete than the person. After the falling away of the human race through sin, it returns through Christ as one Church, one bride. Every breach with God is a breach in the unity of humanity, and can only be repaired by Christ's reconciliation mediated by the Church. This is prefigured in the Bible in Paul's words about the reconciliation of the Jews and the Gentiles to form one body, which is the Church:

> This was to create one single New Man in himself out of the two of them, and by restoring peace through the cross, to unite them both in a single body and reconcile them with God.
> (Ep 2:15–16)

The Book of Revelation offers us a cosmic conclusion, following the fall of Babylon, a symbol of this world under the influence of Satan, when the New Jerusalem, which is a metaphor for the Church glorified, comes as bride for Jesus, who is Alpha and Omega. These are the prophetic images given to us of the end times of God's creation and his plan for human salvation. We saw earlier how, in Isaiah, Babylon is the symbol of idolatry, of the abandonment of God by his people. This is what the world stands accused of today in its apostasy. In his profound reflections on the works of St John, Fr Philippe comments on the meaning of this Babylon of

Revelation (Philippe, 1994, pp. 419–24). He sees it as the scene of the final battle between the forces of good and evil, paralleling the final week of the life of Jesus himself as he moves towards his passion (John 6–11). Now, in Revelation 12 it is the spiritual war between Satan and the Church that is engaged. The dragon and the two beasts of Revelation represent the seduction of the human race into the service of Satan. The work of the two beasts represents the alliance of corrupt intelligence and power, and this is the Babylon that is to be destroyed, the earthly city without God, exactly the creation that Mary points to in her Medjugorje message of 25 January 1997 quoted at the beginning of this chapter.

The first step in the individual's or the community's spiritual journey, therefore, is the destruction of Babylon. Scripture makes this completely clear. The spiritual warfare that rages in our spirits must be resolved before God can reign in us. Or, put simply, we have to recognise the ways in which we have resisted and rejected God, and decide for conversion, before we even seek to approach him. But why should a person decide to bother to respond to the Gospel, when so much is asked? What advantage is there in it? This is a crucial point, since it is the difference between optimism about future conditions, on the one hand, which causes us to calculate relative advantages, personal profit, and so forth and, on the other, belief that our very destiny lies in seeking the truest and best way of being, according to both our own conscience and the teaching of those we have come to trust. In the one case we might decide to do nothing, to regard ourselves as well served by fate, materially comfortable, untroubled by any major anxieties, and happy to assume that things will continue to go well for us. In the latter case we would be searching for the ultimate good, seeing that it requires our entire will, so that our response and our actions stem from our commitment, not from pragmatic calculation.

A journey of the heart

> *That is why I am going to lure her and lead her out into the wilderness, and speak to her heart.'* (Ho 2:16)

In terms of the notion of the spiritual life as a journey which has featured in this book, we could ask: is this journey only a metaphor, an escape from everyday reality, an abstraction leading nowhere? Or could we agree that we are choosing our road with each decision we make for good or evil, to help others or to oppress them? If we take this moral stance about life, then we can say that the journey is no metaphor. It is a daily renewed search, a daily topic of study, reflection and prayer, a daily overcoming of obstacles, many of which are within ourselves. It is therefore a journey that must begin in our own hearts and souls, but which must then extend progressively outwards. The journey that we make through the wilderness of earthly misery towards the heavenly city is thus above all in the spirit. And it is the same for everybody. However we live on earth, in whatever social conditions or with whatever personal make-up, we are all equal in the sight of God. That is, we are none of us more important than anyone else and we are all offered the chance of salvation. And no one is saved except in hope until they have drawn their last breath, because anyone can still choose to turn away. However, even while we are physically in this world, and suffering its trials and confusions, we can be travelling confidently in our hearts towards the final destination. We do this by responding to God, by being true to him, that is to say to his law written in our hearts, our conscience, and guided where necessary by the wisdom and authority of the Church.

The point is that we cannot wait for someone else to assume the responsibility of changing us. It is true that only God and his grace can actually bring about the change, but we have to be willing and ready. This means that we begin the journey out of exile not as a group already formed under a visionary leader, as in the Mosaic times, but in our own spirit. We need to come to a point at which we discard useless elements of the past, our assumptions, desires, habits, and so forth, and decide on a new commitment. However helpless we feel about such an enterprise it is encouraging to realise that ordinary people achieve it all the time. In fact humility has much more to do with personal transformation than great insight. Everyone has a moral conscience that prompts them in their lives. We all have a sense of right and wrong, or better and worse, and conversion begins when we take our own conscience seriously rather than rejecting what it tells us.

The thoughts of exiles who remember their distant homeland are always bitter-sweet. This is very similar to the condition of believers who know that they are temporarily absent from their true home with God. When will they reach their desired destination? How will this be accomplished? How can they keep the faith until that time? Who will help them? The psalms of the exile are very poignant. The Israelites, defeated and captive, languish in Babylon, remembering Sion (Ps 137). They begin to understand that the way back is not by renewing the political struggle, but by resuming the spiritual one. They had been unfaithful to their God, and their exile had come upon them as a just punishment. Only if they can accept their own guilt and responsibility, and so turn back to the worship of God with a new purity, can they continue to hope. This demands a personal conversion and life commitment from each individual, not merely a decision by the leaders. And so it is today. There needs to be a time of turning around in our lives. It may happen early, as it has in the lives of many saints who committed themselves to God from their childhood, or it may happen on the death-bed, as has probably happened to a vastly larger number, but it is a moment of spiritual decision when a person takes moral responsibility for their own life and gives it a definitive direction.

Although I thought I was a convinced Catholic Christian during my youth, and certainly I prayed and hoped for salvation, I can now see that there was a large amount of automatic and mindless following of routines without a genuine personal commitment. It was only much later that I actually chose commitment, but that was the time when I am convinced that my life really began to express something of its true meaning and purpose. I had a sense of the exile coming to an end, of a return to somewhere that I belonged. This did not happen overnight for me, even though the first step was taken on one particular day. After that there was a prolonged time of spiritual discovery, not without pain and confusion. In particular I had to face the fact that my professional life was far more secular in its concerns than I now wanted. I attempted within my university teaching to introduce some new courses on values and the spiritual dimension of life. These had a certain success, but it was difficult to devote to them the time they needed. Eventually I started to write a book on the subject of secular and spiritual values (Plunkett 1990), and it was while writing this book that I came to see that I needed to leave the University to pursue my interests elsewhere. I had no desire actually to stop working, quite the contrary, but it took some time to find a new direction and the new activities which would give me the opportunity to develop my ideas.

During this time the main change was not so much in my work and responsibilities as in my attitude to them. I found that I had a whole new set of criteria for selecting my priorities, and a new motivation in my relationships with students and colleagues. Quite soon my work did evolve, with new courses and research focussed upon values in education. The Maryvale Institute in Birmingham opened up an innovative graduate programme in theological and spiritual studies in which I was able to play a part. This helped me continue my own spiritual journey, while at the same time enabling others to do so. The insight I feel I derived from my experience, and which I hope underlies this book, is the fundamental importance of being willing to go along with God's plans. Even if we are sometimes blessed by a fruitfulness in our efforts this should serve to encourage us without making us presumptuous about our achievements, since they come from God as part of his plan for 'the good employment of our lives' (Ep 2:10).

When, in an earlier chapter, I summarised the spiritual rule that has emerged from Medjugorje, I knew that it had the power to shock even believers by its demands. However, no one can expect to reach the end of a journey straight away, and this journey becomes easier once one begins if we accept the words of the prophets about God's justice replacing his mercy, and his desire that all without exception should be converted in heart and mind without delay. Many have already taken these steps. We do not travel alone, and the Church can guide us by allowing us to enter into communion

Steps in the spiritual life

There is no fixed route for the spiritual journey, but I would rather make some concrete suggestions than simply offer general encouragement. My personal experience suggests the following possibilities, but the main point is to begin and to stay open to the grace that God gives to guide the sincere heart.

- it is abundantly clear from Scripture and the Blessed Virgin's reminders that the essential first step is always prayer
- for Mary, prayer must be of the *heart*, that is, sincere, trusting, and direct, and involving sorrow for our wrongdoing, gratitude to God for our lives and for his promise of salvation, love for him as our Creator, and openness to him about our concerns and needs
- next comes the prayerful reading of Scripture itself, since no Christian life can progress without the word of God, especially the Gospels with the words of Jesus, the other books of the New Testament, and the psalms
- the worship of God can develop with these foundation stones, and further progress can take many forms according to the particular personality, circumstances and needs of the individual concerned and how they are led by the Holy Spirit:

  - meditation on the lives of Jesus and Mary in the rosary
  - contemplative prayer in church before the Blessed Sacrament
  - participation in a Bible study or prayer group
  - patterns of life then begin to change as love of God, other family members and neighbour advance together
  - lifestyles simplify, for example in the area of entertainment
  - a need is felt for a spiritual formation, such as an Alpha course or regular spiritual reading
  - playing a full part in a church community, according to how the individual feels prompted in their heart, including as a Catholic participating in the Mass and sacraments
  - a person who has already travelled some distance might benefit from a pilgrimage, a retreat or from spiritual direction

with others on the same journey. However, we have to aim beyond some lowest common denominator of conversion by which we hope to insure ourselves against the possibility of being rejected by God. What is being asked is commitment and trust in God. The 'how' will vary for each person, but we can say that prayer, conversion, faith, hope in and worship of God, and works of love towards others are the starting-points. The Holy Spirit will lead us on, once we have taken the first steps.

God has not abandoned us, and never will, but we have to place our trust in him as we set out on our return from our particular exile. Our journey is already in his plan, and we have only to cooperate. The redemptive work of Jesus has been accomplished, but its working out in time is not yet complete. This depends upon our response. The Book of Revelation reveals the final triumph of God's purpose. It synthesises and summarises everything that God intends. Thus it recounts the final victory of Jesus Christ, the definitive conquest of Satan, the everlasting reward given to the saints, and the flourishing of the heavenly Jerusalem. It tells us what Heaven want to be heard in its completeness, and declares to us: 'Happy are those who treasure the prophetic message of this book.' (Rv 22:7) Everything that Babylon symbolises is to be destroyed. All that the world vaunts itself for is to be set aside. This does not imply condemnation of individual people, since anyone can be converted and seek pardon, but it must mean that the standards of the world and all its promises and show will be revealed for what they really are, pretence and illusion, and worse than that, a disaster for humanity itself as it runs to its ruin by abandoning the way offered to it in the certain knowledge possessed by the conscience or heart, in which God has written his law, and taught by Jesus Christ and his Church.

10

The message is hope

The people of God

These are the people who have been through the great persecution, and because they have washed their robes white again in the blood of the Lamb, they now stand in front of God's throne and serve him night and day in his sanctuary ...
(Rv 7:13–15)

Prophecy and hope are two aspects of the same thing. The Kingdom of God is a hidden treasure. It is this *already but not yet* quality of salvation that it is so difficult for us to comprehend. Jesus Christ has already saved us by his cross, and yet we ourselves have to ratify his action by living as saved people. If we forget that we are saved and live another way, we lose the benefits won for us. This is why faith that we are saved by the love and sacrifice of Jesus is so important, and why we therefore have to live in hope, the very characteristic of which is to expect what is unseen, up to the point at which we can apprehend it as true when we enter God's Kingdom. Christian hope is not mere optimism,[46] a looking on the bright side, but it is immensely positive; it is the ultimate antidote to everything that threatens life, love and peace. The hope offered by contemporary prophets guided by the Virgin Mary is in fact the complete reversal of the signs of the times with which we began in Chapter One. But we could have understood this from her Magnificat (Lk 1:46–55, which is nothing less than the prophecy of the fall of Babylon, that is, the end of sin, pride and human might and the beginning of mercy to those who fear God, the feeding of the materially and spiritually poor, and the new Covenant brought to fruition.

Obviously, however, there is no such hope unless we make a personal decision for God and for his Kingdom rather than for the values of the world. The Sermon on the Mount clearly describes the commitment that is asked of each one of us. Jesus tells us to live in such a way as to store up treasures in heaven, not on earth. And he speaks that stark and unavoidable truth: 'where your treasure is, there will your heart be also' (Mt 6: 21). Once we have made a new commitment and begun to live in a new way it is likely that we will find that we are simultaneously elated and faltering. The path of our spiritual journey is unsure. We are inexperienced travellers. We have discovered that there is a treasure to seize, and we are confident that it will be ours one day, but we do not yet possess it, nor are we sure of how to find it. Hope, however, is something that has a reason to it, the result essentially of God's promises. As Häring saw in his inspiring book *Hope is the Remedy*, Christian hope is the result of a dialogue with God. We could not have this hope without God:

> Christian hope does not arise from our own yearning or desire, from our own options; if our longing for beatitude has a vital significance, a saving meaning, it is only because God has given it. (Häring, 1971, pp. 29–30)

So it is that even while we are still journeying we can believe that our arrival is assured. This is not presumption, because we are not ascribing the success of our journey to ourselves but to God's promise of mercy.

Along the way, the great counsellor and guide is the Church, the body of Christ. Beyond the veil which hides spiritual realities from impure human eyes, the Church is 'dressed in dazzling white linen' (Rv 19:8). The holiness of the saints and martyrs of the past are as much a part of the Church as the heroism of contemporary sufferers for the faith – and together they make up for the shortcomings of their fellow-Christians. The Church can be soiled or corrupted in one or other respect, but never to the point of being destroyed. Scripture guarantees her survival. The gates of the underworld will never prevail against the Church, however badly its members fail to live up to God's commands. It is for this reason that Christians are required to be true to the Church regardless of the human qualities shown by particular bishops, priests, or other leaders. The saints are those who never lost confidence in the Church, even if they suffered persecution, rejection, or near total misunderstanding by their co-religionaries during their earthly lives. Scores of examples of such humility could be cited, such as that of Padre Pio, the Italian priest mystic, in our own day. For twenty years he was banned from ministry by the Church, but his canonisation as a saint is now a foregone conclusion from what we know of his holy life and the way he was marked by suffering and the stigmata (Gallagher, 1995).

The journey out of exile, though begun in the individual heart or conscience, must become a pilgrimage of the whole Christian community. This is the importance of the Church. Without the Church we are asserting our own autonomy, whereas Christ founded the Church and left it secure upon the earth exactly in order to be a beacon, a guide and a body to which everyone could turn. My return to the Church in this sense was gradual, since it had been partly as a result of rejecting clerical authority and religious conformity that I had abandoned the Church in the 1960's. One important step was the day when I consciously decided to forgive the Church, or rather its representatives, for any ways in which they had oppressed me, and there certainly were some whose zeal had overstepped the mark! Once forgiven, the Church was available to me as a refuge. In fact I came to accept the analogy of the Church as Mother, and I remember feeling intensely moved by Saint Therese's words: 'Au coeur de l'Eglise, ma mère, je serai l'amour'. This seemed to me to sum up the extraordinary power of the Church to centre us, by nourishing us spiritually and reminding us of eternal priorities in a passing world. Thus fed, the people of God become the bride of Christ in the mystical marriage foreshadowed in the Book of Revelation. This imagery of marriage seemed strange to me until I came to understand more fully that God's relationship with us is with our spirit, and earthly marriage is not the model to which spiritual marriage looks. It is the other way round: earthly marriage must look to the model of the spiritual marriage of the soul with God. Indeed, marriage understood this way becomes a very different thing from the faulty legal contract that human society has evolved.

The King of kings

> *I am the Alpha and the Omega, the first and the last, the beginning and the end.* (Rv 22:13)

In a sense the Darwinists are right in thinking that there is a logic to reality, that it is not blind chaos. But according to the light of Christian hope, they have picked the wrong logic. The end, it is true, is in the beginning; there is a close link between the two, because Christ is both beginning and end, Alpha and Omega. What this means, however, is that the direction of our lives is given not by the scientific principle of natural selection, but by the spiritual principle of the truth and love that Jesus taught. The destiny of the whole of humanity is tied up with the life, death and resurrection of Jesus, who is the Word of God, the King of kings, Alpha, who existed from the beginning, and Omega, to whom everything will be made subject at the end. Christ is the reference point for human existence so that no human being can hope for salvation without him, even if they do not know him. Christianity has become so institutionalised that the figure of Jesus has sometimes been obscured. Despite the effects of the Vatican II in enlivening the Catholic Church, it has often been towards new idols that people have turned, and not towards God. Insofar as the whole Christian family comes together around Christ they will surely discover the truth and the unity that has eluded them, and this in turn will be the powerful witness that will bring others swiftly to Christ thereafter. All other ways to God are partial or illusory, and depend for their completeness on Christ. Why should we struggle to interpret Jesus metaphorically when he promises his followers their final arrival at the destination of their journey, not their dissolution into something amorphous in which they will not be able to recollect and know themselves?

This spiritual dimension of reality is like the mighty

iceberg that only has its very tip in this world. Its true proportions are only visible when we go beneath the surface of life. The spiritual can be glimpsed in earthly experience, in our sense of meaning, purpose, relationships, or inner peace. Yet all this will pass away, because we will be disturbed, confused, sick, weak, and finally we will be dead. Is that the end of the spiritual reality? Is that the end of us? We do not know the answers to these questions except in faith. But faith gives us the hope that what is to come is such that our present existence is of little account by comparison. It is this vision, accepted in faith by the individual human heart, that gives a new and vital energy and purpose to our existence on this earth, because it reveals an ultimate destiny beyond death. Our human existence does not end with death. Our spirit lives on to know God in heaven - or to refuse him for eternity. The promise of eternal life contained in the good news of Jesus Christ is unlike the illusory promises of the secular world. Our earthly life is a temporary exile, a time of trial, but it does not last very long. The Book of Revelation tells us that Babylon has already fallen. The world that had rejected God is now itself rejected. We only need to admit this truth to benefit from it, either by adherence to Christian faith or by following our inner conscience faithfully and uncompromisingly, which is everyman's way to holiness and to salvation.

Some have understood the Woman adorned with the sun in Revelation 12, as a symbol of the Church struggling against the satanic figure of the dragon, but Catholic tradition has also seen here a sign of the crucial prophetic and intercessory role played in salvation history by the Blessed Virgin Mary. Just as the Son of God came into the world through Mary so he will return to bring about the final defeat of the powers of darkness through her. The Book of Revelation shows us the outcome, as the devil, in the form of a dragon, attempts to stifle the life of the Church, that is the body of Christ born of the Virgin Mary. This figure of the Woman is chosen by Pope John Paul II to characterise the spiritual struggle between life and death in the world today over abortion and related bio-ethical issues. Mary, especially through her apparitions at Guadalupe in Mexico, is the patroness of the Pro-life movement. She is the declared enemy of abortion, and has promised to bring it to an end. This is an important part of her role in the world today.

Mary's is the life that most fully responded to its Creator of all the creatures that have ever existed. There is no shadow of sin in her. That is why we can follow her in a way that we could not follow even a saint. In the case of Mary we hardly need discernment, and then only to guard us from our own errors. A remarkable Italian mystic, Luisa Piccaretta, who died in 1947, and was almost totally unknown until very recently, has left a massive written record of a whole spirituality based upon the model of Mary's life as someone who lived in the Kingdom of the divine will, that is, someone who constantly chose God's will rather than her own (Piccarreta, 1995). This apparently very demanding discipline is shown to provide the key to understanding the call of the Gospel. Jesus says to Luisa:

> My daughter, in order for the soul to be able to forget herself, everything she does or has to do must be done as if I wanted to do it in her. If she prays, she should say: 'It is Jesus who wants to pray, and I pray together with him.' If she works: 'It is Jesus who wants to work ...' (p.124).

Indeed, if one sentence could sum up the spirituality that Heaven is calling for, it might be something very similar to the message of *When the Divine Will Reigns in Souls*: holiness, salvation, and eternal life consist in living the will of God in preference to our own desires, just as Jesus taught in the words of his prayer: 'Thy will be done on earth, as it is in heaven'.

The new Jerusalem

> *I saw the holy city, and the new Jerusalem, coming down from God out of heaven, as beautiful as a bride all dressed for her husband.* (Rv 21:2)

The final chapters of the Book of Revelation are full of prophetic images of completeness: the city of God, the pure river running through the heart of the city and the healing leaves of the trees that line it, the wiping away of tears, the crowds streaming through the gates of paradise, and the consummation of the mystical marriage between Christ, the Lamb of God, and his Church. This is not sentiment, but the living out of faith, hope and love, the main virtues taught by Jesus. While the contemporary prophets speak to us of a new era of peace, I believe that they are still not speaking of the new Jerusalem. To understand the new Jerusalem we have to turn to the Book of Revelation with faith and discernment. Like Jesus and the saints whom we see portrayed there in their glorious state, we have to go through life and death to know the new life of the heavenly Jerusalem. Along the way there may be encouraging signposts and symbols, such as an era of peace, or the conversion of peoples to faith in God foretold by some of the contemporary prophets, but this is not the final point of arrival. God promises us *eternal* salvation. That is what his prophets today call us to believe in, to proclaim and to live, and to work for as our ultimate destiny. This can be done in prayerful silence and recollection or in strenuous secular activity, provided only that we seek and follow God's will. He has a distinct plan for each one, but the essential character of his plan is that we seek and welcome his will, that we live in his will rather than in our own, that we fully trust in him rather than in ourselves or any human formula. There, where Scripture, the Church and the modern prophets are aligned, we find the spiritual wisdom to lead our lives in holiness.

The conclusion that each is obliged to reach involves a risk, and a decision to trust. For the Christian it is a decision to trust Jesus, since the promises of Christianity were given to us by Jesus. For the agnostic it may be a question of whether to decide to trust Jesus more than Western secular values, and whether to decide to hope that we will find life after death. This is not a selfish option, as is sometimes alleged against believers. It is of the very nature of religious belief that humanity reflects God, that the best human qualities are mirror images of the qualities of the Creator (cf. 2 Co 3:18), and therefore we cannot conceive of God as having favourites but only as giving to all the chance to know him and to enjoy life with him after death, unless we freely choose to refuse his gift. Anyone who doubts that such promises exist has only to open the Bible at Revelation 3 and read the sublime passage about Jesus standing at our door, knocking, and offering to enter into our hearts and share his throne with us. This then is our destination. We can speak of it in spiritual terms as holiness, in literal terms as paradise, or in symbolic terms as the new Jerusalem. This new city, symbol of the Kingdom and the antithesis of the Babylon that has fallen, shines forth in the last book of Scripture. This is because everything in it relates to our coming to God, our entering his Kingdom. The new Jerusalem is the heavenly city, where there is no need for the sun because it is lit by the presence of God, and it is there that the blessed will live in eternity after having passed through the tribulations of life on earth (Rv 7:14). These consolations of the Book of the Apocalypse were dramatically demonstrated by the apparition at Knock, Ireland, on 21 August 1879, at a time when the people of that country were suffering from widespread misery and famine. Heaven's voice spoke through a silent vision to a whole people. I cite this particularly because the vision also expresses and illuminates the link being made in this book between Scripture, Church and prophecy.

The vision at Knock

The vision appeared for two hours on the gable end of a church, and was seen by fifteen people ranged from six to seventy five years.

- the vision took the form of an immobile tableau composed of Mary, crowned as Queen of Heaven, and the three male figures with whom she shared her earthly life: St Joseph, Jesus, and St John.
- Mary was in an attitude of contemplative prayer
- St Joseph, the Protector of the Holy Family, was in an attentive attitude of interceding prayer
- St John, dressed as a bishop, was preaching the saving word of Scripture
- Jesus was portrayed as the Lamb of God upon an altar, the victim eternally sacrified for our redemption

Many are called to be prophets

> *When they take you before synagogues and magistrates and authorities, do not worry about how to defend yourselves or what to say, because when the time comes, the Holy Spirit will teach you what you must say.* (Lk 12:11)

If we receive Heaven's messages humbly we cannot fail to be moved by them, since they tell us what our inner consciences already know, namely, that we have gone astray, that we have spoiled the world, dissipated our lives in selfish and material pleasure, and taken a utilitarian and short-term view of our existence. The appeal the messages make to us is to reconsider our relationship to our Creator, to repudiate our wrongdoing, to open our hearts to God's forgiveness and love, and to live according to the light he has given us in the Gospel and in the life of Jesus the incarnate God. This is what people need to hear, and what Heaven wants, but everything depends upon the obedience of the believers, the humility of the hearers, and ultimately the conscience of the inviolate human person. This is an awesome truth: God respects each one of us absolutely, and leaves our fate to our own choice. However, we cannot say that we were not warned, or that the message was too complicated to understand, because the warnings of the prophets are coming thick and fast, so as to reach every corner of the globe and every kind of person, Christian and non-Christian alike.

However, the Gospel is also a call to all to 'Go and make disciples of all the nations' (Mt 28:19), and this too needs a response in each heart and in each life. Everyone will be judged according to their response. God desires that we call one another; that we understand that we have a responsibility towards one another, that we are our brother's keeper. Likewise, the Blessed Virgin in Medjugorje asks us to be the messengers of her messages. This task is not of course confined to the Medjugorje messages. It means that many are called to have the faith to be prophets, to listen to messages claimed to be from Heaven, and to decide if they feel prompted by the Spirit to share them with others. And those who are given the opportunity to share them more widely have a greater responsibility to discern and to act. Such a great responsibility should not cause us worry, however, because it is the Holy Spirit who will teach us what to say when the time comes.

I am entirely convinced by my own study of the Scriptures, by my understanding of the perennial teaching of the Church, and by my consciousness of the confirmatory messages of the contemporary prophets that God is calling the world to a change of mind and heart. He is revealing his deep sadness at the widespread atheism, the scorn for his commandments, and the refusal to submit to his benign authority and to his perfect plan for his creation. He could simply leave us to our own devices, and in the fullness of time show us through his final judgement where we have gone wrong. That would be too late for our conversion, and would mean the loss of many souls to hell. He could reverse his decision to leave us free in conscience, and simply correct us, or frighten us into submission. I say he 'could', but in fact this would be against his nature, for he decided already to leave us free, and God cannot change his mind. The only other possibility is that he could warn us in such a way as to prompt us to change without forcing us. Such warnings would be clear and unambiguous, but would only be compelling for us in so far as we actually hear them, are open to them, and are ready to obey our own consciences. This is what I believe is now happening.

How then are we to reflect this conversion in our lives? Do we not have to become prophets ourselves? And prophets, not of doom, but of hope? As far as the world is concerned there has never been such a need of hope, and of witness to hope (John Paul II, 1994). If the new pagans revere the world for its inherent beauty, Christians revere it more, because they believe it was created by a loving God to fulfil his plan and to manifest his glory. If secular humanists acclaim human rights to justice, then Christians believe that human dignity must be inviolate, because they believe that human nature is created by God in his image. If New Agers are hopeful because of their conviction that we are entering the astrological age of Aquarius, then Christians have even more hope because they believe that Jesus died and rose again to win eternal salvation for all who call upon him. The theme of hope is what Christians and all believers in divine Providence should take to the world, not to justify the world as it is, but to evoke a response of love to its merciful Creator.

The message is thus one of hope for all, not a secret for the few. Those who come to knowledge and belief have the way to heaven open to them. They receive the road-map for salvation; the way of life preached by Jesus Christ, one which has never been rescinded, and which has only two direction signs: love of God and love of neighbour. These are the principles that help to plan the journey, and which resolve all problems on the road. Just as 'dangerous bend' causes the moral driver to slow down, so the instruction given in the Sermon on the Mount: 'love your enemies, and pray for those who persecute you' or 'do not commit adultery' causes the Christian to restrain dangerous impulses. This is not repressive, but the way to a fuller life, one that can expand to eternity instead of narrowing to its own immediate gratification. The constant choice for God, for life, and for love, is the path indicated by the genuine prophets, and the way to spiritual growth and to life with God. There is no greater wisdom, no superior truth, no fuller freedom than in living this way of love. If we do not already know this, then that is the message that Heaven wants to be heard, and it is the message that authentic prophets have always proclaimed: God's amazing generosity to a world that has treated him with such indifference and even rejection. All we have to do is to echo Mary's 'Let it be'.

The prayer that has accompanied this writing

Come, Holy Spirit, as you came to the apostles.
Open our minds that we may see the hidden things of God.
Send love into our hearts, like a flame of fire,
that our lives may be changed by the power of your Spirit,
to do God's will on earth,
and bring others with us to heaven.

Epilogue

I have written this book out of the growing conviction that a moral and spiritual darkness is afflicting the world, while at the same time there are signs that are daily becoming clearer that God is offering light to those who wish to see. I must reemphasise that I strongly believe that the necessary light is already given in the Scriptures and through the Church, and that most of what I have had to say in this book is by way of a reminder of what we should know, or could know if we take the written word of God and the teaching of the Church seriously. In focussing this book upon the messages of contemporary prophets, it has not been my intention to create any sensation of a fundamentalist nature regarding catastrophes that are said to be set to occur in the world. Instead, my main contention is that these messages are *first and foremost* a call for a return to God, for a spiritual renewal of lives and cultures. I do believe that there is a great risk in neglecting this appeal, but this is no more than the Scriptures tell us: that there will be a judgement. If, along the way to this final tribunal, therefore, incidents occur that bring us up short, and alarm us, these cannot be seen as actions of a vengeful God, but rather the warnings of a patient and loving Father who desires to see the fulfilment of his plans for creation in peace and goodness. This paragraph really contains all I have to say, only it has taken me sixty years to learn to say it!

As for the teaching of the Catholic Church to which I belong, and to which I hope always to remain faithful, I endorse its taking a cautious and prudent approach to mystical and other supernatural phenomena. However, the Church has always recognised the reminders of God's promises to be found in the lives of its saints and other holy people. So, today, miracles continue to occur, in conversions, healings and visions, no doubt associated in many cases with people who will one day be recognised as saints. These are a part of Catholic consciousness because the Church is built upon hope for things unseen.

As I finish this writing, and reflect on the journey so far and imagine what is to come, I have two sources of sadness that still afflict me. The first is that I personally travelled by such an indirect route to get to where I am, when really it was so simple. The road-map had been handed to me as a child, and is perhaps handed in some dimly perceived way to every child. And the second sadness is that there seem to be so many people who cannot find the resolve in themselves to consider God's promises and to ask him to include them in his mercy, despite all the teaching, the evidence of spiritual renewal, and the amazing manifestations of Heaven attested by modern prophets.

But I also have two consolations. The first is that it does not matter to God if we travel by an indirect route, so long as we arrive at the destination of knowing and loving him. The Christian way simply makes this journey easier and more direct. And my second consolation is that the world has not yet ended, but the victory of Jesus over sin and death has already taken place. God's plan is still in force, a plan to win us, not by obligation or manipulation but by love and mercy, and that is the hope I still have and want to hold out to other travellers on the road.

Notes

1 The passages of Scripture that head sections of the book essentially illustrate but do not explore one of the 'three legs' of the stool, and are included rather than being merely referenced, for those without a bible to hand. Citations are nearly all taken from the Jerusalem Bible and follow the abbreviations and format it uses.

2 *Gaudium et Spes*, para 4. As there are a number of references to the Second Vatican Council, it may be helpful to those unfamiliar with its documents to explain that they are all gathered into one volume (Flannery, 1988), but distinguished by their Latin titles.

3 To illustrate this, two highly acclaimed social analysts, the sociologist Charles Handy and the economist Will Hutton, make good use of their talents in social and economic analysis, but both fail to acknowledge any place for God in, or any spiritual significance to their task of seeking the way to a better future (Handy, 1995; Hutton, 1995). Handy, though a Christian, appears to find this of no relevance to his book. Hutton believes in the possibility of centre left politics giving us solutions, and allocates an important place to values, but no place to a source of values.

4 cf. Brown, 1992, an example of a new genre of writing, popularising private revelation, but with the attendant dangers of superficiality, sensationalism, and putting off those who most need to hear an authentic message. He

uses a question and answer format, and this results in a very personal treatment of the topics; and Thompson, 1996, a work that spreads itself very wide, and lumps together all kinds of manifestations. The result is that matters that are of great significance to the Catholic Church are tarred with the same brush, and treated superficially, or with a tongue in cheek manner.

5 The Pope wrote in these terms in his first encyclical letter (*Redemptor Hominis*, para 1) and the theme was still there in his most recent letter at the time of writing (*Tertio Millennio Adveniente*, para 23).

6 The gap in the British literature in however beginning to be filled by the series of books by the Chief Rabbi, Jonathan Sacks, including his most recent work on hope (see Sacks, 1997)

7 As Pope John Paul puts it in *Veritatis Splendor* (John Paul, 1993): 'The individual conscience is accorded the status of a supreme tribunal of moral judgement which hands down categorical and infallible decisions about good and evil' (para 32).

8 See Cole et al.,1990, an informative collection of articles by well-known Protestant writers, which presents the New Age as 'an international network of many different groups, encompassing the occult, Eastern religions and Western humanism' (p. 96).

9 England, 1990, discusses the New Age movement and its incursions into the Catholic Church through such phenomena as feminism, creation-centred spirituality Eastern mysticism and meditation techniques, the occult and humanistic psychology.

10 There is a grave problem of discernment here for Church authorities and for all believers, as can be seen from the enthusiasm that characterises the followers of the former Dominican, Matthew Fox, with his creation-centred spirituality (cf. Fox, 1983).

11 Barker, 1989, offers detailed research on New Religious Movements, but without a moral and spiritual discernment which would reveal the true nature of satanic as opposed to simply misguided tendencies.

12 Apart from the *Catechism* (Catechism of the Catholic

Church, 1994), which is a mine of doctrinal and biblical teaching, this and the following chapter could be usefully extended by a reading of John Redford's powerful exposition of his answers to what he has called 'Hard Questions' (see Redford, 1996).

[13] The Vatican II declaration on Scripture, *Dei Verbum* , and the *Catechism* indicate the main relevant Catholic teachings (Flannery, 1988, and *Catechism of the Catholic Church*).

[14] O'Brien, 1996, portrays many of these issues through a novel, but one which reflects deep knowledge of the Church and many of the same preoccupations that underlie this book. In particular the novelist sees the Church divided, and this division exploited by a mysterious figure, greatly admired by nearly all the world, but gradually exposed as a satanic personality, the antichrist. The conversation between the Pope and the dissident Cardinal Vettore (pp. 500–513) is a masterly summary of the issues of papal authority and the claims of the 'collegialists'.

[15] The historian Paul Johnson has written a vigorous and very well-informed personal testimony to his faith in, and reasoned explanation of the Catholic Church (Johnson, 1997, Chapter 10 'The church, dogma, authority, order and liturgy')

[16] I am reassured by the collection of testimonies, *Surprised by Truth*, of a number of American Evangelicals who, through often lengthy but rigorously honest search, came to discover the scriptural authority of the Catholic Church and its infallible guiding by the Holy Spirit as the fulfilment of Christ's promises (Madrid, 1995).

[17] It is not part of this book to survey internal theological disputes, but there is undoubtedly a fundamental debate in the Church over the status of papal authority. An American initiative, the Catholic Common Ground Project, begun under the leadership of Cardinal Bernardin who died in late 1996, has issued a statement entitled 'Called to be Catholic', which hints at compromise rather than defending revealed truth. It includes the contentions: 'We should recognise that no single group or viewpoint in the Church has a complete monopoly on the truth' and

'We should test all proposals for their pastoral realism and potential impact on living individuals as well as for their theological truth.' The statement was criticised by Cardinal Law as making 'truth and dissent from truth equal partners in ecclesiastical dialogue' (*The Tablet*, 17 August 1996).

[18] Such a dogma, one that would include the role of co-redemptrix, could well be proclaimed, and is in fact currently the subject of a world-wide petition to the Pope. Mark Miravalle,1993, has spearheaded a movement to petition the Pope to declare the dogmas of Mary Co-redemptrix, Mediatrix of Graces, and Advocate, and has also edited a theological work that seeks to provide the underpinnings for this proposed teaching.

[19] I was impressed and moved by Eamonn Duffy's scholarly work in which he shows, by reference to Church art and architectural history, how much violence was done to consciences during the Reformation in England. The traditional faith had to be crushed as a matter of political expediency, but in fact was never totally crushed (Duffy, 1992).

[20] Helpful discussions of discernment in relation to private revelation are given by Laurentin (Laurentin, 1995, Part 1) and more generally in relation to prophecy, by Yocum (Yocum,1993, chap. 8).

[21] Mgr George Tüttő has provided a very valuable course of meditations based upon the messages of Medjugorje related to scriptural texts (see Tüttő, 1991).

[22] Thompson, 1996, includes very percipient comments on the Pope's attitude to the Millennium, but he gives Catholic prophets some strange company. It is a pity also that he treats Marian devotion as 'traditionalist' rather than prophetic, and that he identifies 'Marian enthusiasts' rather than their faith and prayer. This said, Thompson is judicious in his assessment of Marian prophecies: 'the Virgin's warnings are not crudely millennarian' (p. 178); and: 'devotion to the Virgin Mary has, throughout Catholic history, represented a route by which apocalyptic belief has entered the Church through the back door.... the cult depends heavily upon traditions and beliefs which

have not been imposed by the Church but which, on the contrary, the faithful have imposed ...' (p. 176).

23 These messages are privately published, but widely available in many languages (See Marian Movement of Priests, 1995).

24 Hill, 1995, belongs to the Protestant tradition of writing on prophecy. He combines scriptural and sociological perspectives, and sees a moral dimension to a 'succession of manmade and natural disasters' (p.92). There is an effort to tie current world events into biblical prophecies of the 'shaking of the nations' which he sees as giving a meaning and purpose to history (p. 187). However, he says that the Church is not ready for battle because its leaders have failed to understand the signs of the times.... The result is that the Church is unable to interpret contemporary history' (p. 203–4). Hope of the voice of the prophet being heard lies with the Evangelicals (p. 206). There is no recognition of the prophetic voice of the Virgin Mary through her current apparitions.

25 The CDF defends the truth of the Catholic faith by censoring misleading or erroneous statements claiming to be Catholic. Thus it issued a statement warning of the dangers of an overly Marxist Liberation Theology, and it warns where it finds theological or other evidence of the inauthenticity of claimed miraculous events, revelations, etc.

26 Sr Emmanuel, 1995, gives a careful listing of names of senior Church figures who have privately given their approval to Medjugorje. These include nearly one hundred bishops who have visited Medjugorje, thirty-five who have not been there, and some of their testimonies, including some from the Pope, such as: ' Medjugorje is the fulfilment and continuation of Fatima'. The book also contains the text of the Yugoslav Bishops' Conference *Declaration* on Medjugorje.

27 See especially the cited works by Laurentin, Brown, and the Flynns, but also the corpus of Laurentin's work of over one hundred books! Laurentin, 1995, provides one of the most useful reference works in the field, a book that lists scores of apparitions, and gives some basic informa-

tion about each. He also concludes with a discussion of the key points of the messages. The book by the Flynns is one of the most valuable attempts to gather together information in English about a wide range of contemporary private revelations, discussed from the perspective of believers and without undue hype.

28 The contested cases of Garabandal and Vassula both have many convinced followers, and the official grounds for questioning them have not yet been made known. In order not to mislead the reader I felt it necessary to be as clear as I can be about the status of these claimed private revelations in the eyes of Catholic Church authorities. Any further discernment belongs to the individual guided, in the case of Catholic believers, by the Church. In reviewing the very profuse literature of private revelations it helps to have in mind that, at least from the Catholic standpoint, it is prudent to pay more attention to those messages which come from approved revelations, or to those which have survived a lengthy period without being rejected, than to messages which are seriously questioned by Church authorities. Private revelations that have been officially and definitively condemned should of course be treated extremely circumspectly by a Catholic, and certainly not be in any way promoted. It is not my understanding, however, that the Church's warnings concerning either Garabandal or Vassula amount to condemnation.

29 Fr Gobbi's messages endorse nearly all these spiritual appeals, but especially for prayer and for consecration to the Immaculate Heart of Mary. In fact, his first message, or 'locution', was received in 1981 at Fatima, the main source of contemporary devotion to Mary's Immaculate Heart.

30 This devotion has been practised nearly all his life by Pope John Paul II, and he recommends it to everyone in his encyclical *Redemptoris Mater*.

31 All the spiritual appeals included in the chart occur in Vassula's messages. Her messages, however, reflect one overwhelming priority: the return of the Churches, Catholic, Orthodox and Protestant, to unity. Also, with their notable spiritual content, especially regarding the

Sacred Heart of Jesus and the Holy Spirit, the messages are concerned with the intimate relationship of the soul to its Creator. Though a Greek Orthodox, Vassula speaks of the primacy of the Bishop of Rome, as well as of devotions to the rosary and to the Sacred Heart of Jesus and the Immaculate Heart of Mary, which are foreign to Orthodox spirituality. One of the most intriguing appeals in her messages, as in those of the Syrian visionary Mirna, is for the unifying of the dates of Easter by the Eastern and Western churches. According to a prophecy in Vassula's messages, help will eventually come from the East to bring about the Church's revival and the reconciliation of its Eastern and Western branches.

[32] Birch, 1996, has researched the history of private revelation, especially related to the antichrist, throughout the Christian era up to the early twentieth century, and he also gives attention to relevant Church teaching and tradition. The book concentrates on prophecies of the antichrist, and Birch maintains that their fulfilment must still be a long way off, since he argues that there has first to be a time of peace which has not yet occurred. Unfortunately, Birch ignores the voice of Heaven in our time, dismissing unapproved prophecy as being equivalent to false prophecy. But what is striking is that the earlier prophecies he cites (the coming of the antichrist, wars, the sacking of Rome, the flight and murder of the Pope, chastisements and the three days of darkness) are repeated so many times in the course of the centuries - often by saints - that recent private revelations offer little new content, only new relevance.

[33] cf. letter written to Pope John Paul II by Fr Tomislav Vlasic, Mirjana's spiritual director, in 1983 (reprinted in O'Carroll,1986).

[34] The eleventh English edition of *To the Priests, Our Lady's Beloved Sons*, 1995, contains nearly 700 pages.

[35] The similar warnings of Vassula's messages speak of the unfaithfulness of the ministers, the pride of spiritual leaders, and rebellion against the Magisterium of the Church by scholars, one of whom will be installed on the throne of Peter and will make changes to God's laws and

traditions, especially those concerning the Eucharistic Sacrifice.

[36] The justification for including these very strong prophecies here is that they are so consistent for many different messengers.

[37] In early 1997, the weeping of the Civitavecchia statue was declared to be an authentic miracle by a commission of theologians appointed by the local bishop.

[38] In my own book on Medjugorje, published in March 1990 before anyone began to expect hostilities in Yugoslavia, I referred to messages about Satan wanting to destroy and lurking in the desert, while Medjugorje was said by the Virgin Mary to be an 'oasis of peace' (Plunkett, 1990, p.40).

[39] This was one of the best known prophecies of the contested Garabandal private revelations of the 1960's.

[40] In an extraordinary acknowledgement of the contemporary significance of such phenomena, the Vatican newspaper published a series of six articles on sects and satanic cults viewed from various aspects: psychological, anthropological, doctrinal, pastoral, etc. See *Osservatore Romano* (English language weekly edition), nos 5–10, 1997.

[41] The Spirit is the source of our renewal and the revealer of heavenly wisdom and mysteries. Although I have acknowledged the objections raised concerning Vassula's writings by the CDF, I believe that they refer to specific points that have yet to be indicated. It seems unlikely to me that the following passage, about the nature of the Holy Spirit, could attract censure. This lyrical and poetic message is inspiring, and even if we only see it as the result of Vassula's 'personal meditations' it opens up dimensions of our understanding of the third person of the Trinity.

> I will ... replace all that hindered my passage in you by the One whom you thought unattainable; he will be the light of your eyes, the motive of your being, the movement of your heart, the utterance of your speech, your laughter and your joy, the kingly adornment of your soul, the watchman of your spirit; he will be your brother, your sister and your

faithful friend; he will be your festivity, your banquet, the hidden treasure, the pearl, your hymn to the Hymn, your amen to the Amen, the promised land and the foundation of all virtues on which he will inscribe his holy name. (Ryden, 1996, pp. 41–42)

[42] Martin, 1994, discusses the conflicts in the Catholic Church worldwide, but in order to identify its need to change, the contribution to be made by the Holy Spirit and the charismatic renewal, and the need for a prophetic Church. This is a visionary book, full of information and farsighted ideas, as well as being open to prophecy and to the special role given by God to the Virgin Mary.

[43] See Lenoir, 1988, for his abundant insights into the new communities by a method of penetrating interviews with their principal figures. These include several names that figure prominently in the renewal of the Church in France, such as Fr Philippe, Jean Vanier, Fr Daniel Ange and Br Ephraim.

[44] Ferguson, 1982, an encyclopaedia of the developing New Age movement, anticipates a transformation of consciousness as the Age of Aquarius begins.

[45] See Cox, 1884, who revises the view he had earlier taken in *The Secular City* that religion was being stifled by secularisation. Now he sees signs that this movement is being reversed.

[46] This point, which appears to me to be a key one for the believer, is developed by Jonathan Sacks in *The Politics of Hope* (Sacks, 1997).

Bibliography and privately published sources

Books

Barker, E. *New Religious Movements* (London, HMSO, 1989)

Bartholomew, C. *A Scientist Researches Mary, the Ark of the Covenant* (Asbury, NJ, 101 Foundation, 1995)

Bernardin, Cardinal J. et al. *Called to be Catholic* (New York, National Pastoral Life Center, 1996)

Birch, D. A. *Trial, Tribulation and Triumph: Before, During and After Antichrist* (Santa Barbara, CA, Queenship Pub. Co., 1996)

Bloom, A. *The Closing of the American Mind* (Harmondsworth, Penguin, 1998)

Brown, M.H. *The Final Hour* (Milford, Ohio, Faith Publishing Co., 1992)

Brown, M.H. *The Day Will Come* (Ann Arbor, Michigan, Servant Publications, 1996)

Cole, M., Higton, T., Graham, J., Lewis, D.C. *What is the New Age?* (London, Hodder, 1990)

Cox, H. *Religion in the Secular City* (New York, Simon and Schuster, 1984)

Croissant, Ephraim *Marthe* (Nouan-le-Fuzelier, Eds du Lion de Juda, 1990)

Cupitt, D. *The Sea of Faith* (London, BBC, 1984)

Cupitt, D. *After All: Religion without Alienation* (London, SCM, 1994)

Daniel-Ange *Guetteur! le Cri de la Nuit, l'Entends-tu?* (Paris, Fayard, 1993)

Davies, N. *Europe: a History* (Oxford, OUP, 1996)

Dove, J. *Strange Vagabond of God: the History of John Bradburne* (Swords, Ireland, Poolbeg, 1993)

Duffy, E. *The Stripping of the Altars: Traditional Religion in England* (Newhaven, Yale U. Press, 1992)

England, R. *Unicorn in the Sanctuary: the Impact of the New Age on the Catholic Church* (Manassas, Virginia, Trinity Communications, 1990)

Ferguson, M. *The Aquarian Conspiracy: Personal and Social Transformation in the 1980's* (London, Granada, 1982)

Fernandez-Armesto, F. *Millennium: a History of our Last Thousand Years* (London, Transworld Publishers, 1996)

Flynn, T. and M. *The Thunder of Justice: the Warning, the Miracle, the Chastisement, the Era of Peace* (Sterling, Va, MaxKol Communications, 1993)

Fox, M. *Original Blessing: a Primer in Creation Spirituality* (Santa Fe, New Mexico, Bear and Co., 1983)

Gallagher, J. *Padre Pio: the Pierced Priest* (Harper Collins, 1995)

Handy, C. *The Empty Raincoat: Making Sense of the Future* (Arrow Books, 1995)

Häring, B. *Hope is the Remedy* (Slough, St Paul Publications, 1971)

Hill, C. *Shaking the Nations* (Eastbourne, Kingsway, 1995)

Hobsbawm, E. *Age of Extremes: the Short Twentieth Century, 1914–1991* (London: Abacus, 1995)

Hogan, F. *Words of Life from John the Beloved* (London, Collins Fount, 1988)

Hutton, W. *The State We're In* (London, Cape, 1995)

Johnson, P. *The Quest for God: a Personal Pilgrimage* (London, Phoenix, 1997)

Laurentin, R. *L'Eglise qui Vient: au-delà des Crises* (Paris, Desclée, 1989)

Laurentin, R. *Multiplication des Apparitions de la Vierge Aujourd'hui* (Paris, Fayard, 1995)

Laurentin, R. *When God Gives a Sign* (Independence, Missouri, Trinitas, 1987)

Laurentin, R. and Joyeux, H. *Scientific and Medical Studies of the Apparitions at Medjugorje* (Dublin, Veritas, 1987)
Lenoir, F. *Les Communautés Nouvelles* (Paris, Fayard, 1988)
Lubac, H.de *Catholicism* (London, Burns, Oates and Washbourne, 1950)
Martin R. *The Catholic Church at the End of an Age* (San Francisco, Ignatius, 1994)
McKenzie, J.L. *Dictionary of the Bible* (London, Chapman, 1968)
Miravalle, M.I., ed. *Mary, Coredemptix, Mediatrix, Advocate: Theological Foundations* (Santa Barbara, CA, Queenship Publishing, 1995)
Moltmann, J. *Theology of Hope: on the Ground and the Implications of a Christian Eschatology* (London, SCM, 1967)
Montfort, St Louis Marie de *True devotion to Mary* (Rockford, Ill, Tan, 1985)
Neuhaus, R.J. *The Catholic Moment* (New York, Harper and Row, 1987)
O'Brien, M. *Fr Elijah: an Apocalypse* (San Francisco, Ignatius, 1996)
O'Carroll, M. *Medjugorje: Facts, Documents, Theology* (Dublin, Veritas, 1986)
Philippe, M.D. *Les Trois Sagesses* (Paris, Fayard, 1994)
Piccarreta, Luisa *When the Divine Will Reigns in Souls* (Jacksonville, Florida, Luisa Piccarreta Center for the Divine Will, 1995)
Pingault, P. *Renouveau de l'Eglise: les Communautés Nouvelles* (Paris, Fayard, 1989)
Plunkett, D. *Queen of Prophets: the Spiritual Message of Medjugorje* (London, Darton, Longman and Todd, 1990)
Plunkett, D. *Secular and Spiritual Values: Grounds for Hope in Education* (London, Routledge, 1990)
Redford, J. *Catholicism: Hard Questions* (London, Chapman, 1997)
Sacks, J. *The Politics of Hope* (London, Cape, 1997)
Teilhard de Chardin, P. *The Phenomenon of Man* (Harper and Row, 1959)
Terelya, J. *Witness to Apparitions and Persecution in the USSR: an Autobiography* (Milford, Ohio, Faith Publishing

Co., 1991)
Thompson, D. *The End of Time: Faith and Fear in the Shadow of the Millennium* (London, Sinclair-Stevenson, 1996)
Yocum, B. *Prophecy: Exercising the Prophetic Gifts of the Spirit in the Church Today* (Ann Arbor, Michigan, Servant, revised edition, 1993)

Scripture

Jerusalem Bible (London, Darton, Longman and Todd, 1968)

Church and papal documents

Catechism of the Catholic Church (London, Chapman, 1994)
Congregation for the Doctrine of the Faith *Instruction on Christian Freedom and Liberation* (Vatican, CDF, 1986)
Congregation for the Doctrine of the Faith *Instruction on the Ecclesial Vocation of the Theologian* (Vatican, CDF, 1990)
Flannery, A., ed. Vatican Council II: The Conciliar and Post-Conciliar Documents (New York, Costello, 1990)
John Paul II *Redemptor Hominis* (Catholic Truth Society, 1979)
Dominum et Vivificantem (Catholic Truth Society, 1986)
Redemptoris Mater (Catholic Truth Society, 1991)
Veritatis Splendor (Catholic Truth Society, 1993)
Crossing the Threshold of Hope (Jonathan Cape, 1994)
Tertio Millennio Adveniente (Catholic Truth Society, 1994)
Evangelium Vitae (Catholic Truth Society, 1995)
Paul VI *Marialis Cultus* (Catholic Truth Society, 1974)

Private or non-commercial publications

(in which data on particular contemporary prophecies can be found)

General:

Pittsburg Center for Peace, *Our Lady, Queen of Peace* (Special Edition 1, Winter 1992; Special Edition 2, Winter 1993; Special Edition 3, Spring 1995)

see also: Brown, 1992; Laurentin,1995; Flynn, T. and M.,1993

Betania, 1976:

Bartholomew,1995, chap. 29

Christina Gallagher:

Petrisko, T.W. (1995) *The Sorrow, the Sacrifice and the Triumph: the Apparitions, Visions and Prophecies of Christina Gallagher* (privately published)

Vincent, R. *Please come Back to Me and my Son* (Ireland's Eye Publications, 1992)

Gobbi, Fr Stefano:

To the Priests, Our Lady's Beloved Sons (Marian Movement of Priests, 11th English edition, 1995)

Kibeho:

Derobert (no initial), *Le Ciel Descend-il a Kibeho?* (Marquain, Editions Hovine, 1984)

Medjugorje:

Maillard, Sr Emmanuel and Nolan, D. *Medjugorje and the Church* (Notre Dame, Indiana, United for the Triumph of the Immaculate Heart, 1995)

Tüttő, George *Living the Gospel with Our Lady* (London, privately published, 1991)

Mir Magazine, Manchester Medjugorje Centre

see also: O'Carroll, 1986; Plunkett, 1990; Laurentin and Joyeux, 1987

Patricia:
The Way of Divine Innocence (newsletter, published by the Divine Innocence Trust, Surbiton, London)

Two Patricks:
Rushe, Patrick and O'Kane, Patrick (the two Patricks) *An Invitation to Love Jesus* (Cookstown, N.Ireland, 1996)
Invitation to love Jesus (newsletter published the Sacred Heart House of Prayer, Cookstown, N.Ireland)

Renato Baron, Schio, Italy:
Mary is Calling (Opera di Amore, Schio, Italy, c. 1995)

Vassula:
Ryden, Vassula, *True Life in God* (Belfast: JMJ Publications) successive volumes continuing up to time of writing
see also: Laurentin, 1993

Note:
For stock-lists of privately and non-commercially published material relating to contemporary private revelations, contact the following:

Centre for Peace, Cardinal Heenan Centre, High Road, Ilford, Essex IG1 1QP
Marian Spring Books, Unit J, Lambs Business Park, Tilburstow Hill Road, S. Godstone, Surrey RH9 8JZ.

Index